Fourth Party Logistics: The Future Of Supply Chain Outsourcing?

Author: Şerafettin Kutlu

University Of Salford

Salford Business School

The Future Of Supply Chain Outsourcing?

Published by:
Best Global Publishing Ltd
PO Box 9366
Brentwood
Essex
CM13 1ZT
United Kingdom

www.bestglobalpublishing.com

Acknowledgements

First and foremost, the author would like to thank his supervisor Dr. John Davies for his help, ideas and suggestions during the course of this research. This dissertation would not have reached this point without his support.

The author is also thankful for Andrew Latchford, the director of VP Group Ltd. in Essex, UK for his genuine interest in this research and significant contribution to the case study. He spared his time for the interview and gave valuable ideas about the topic. The author would also like thank the CEO Jason Pegler of Chipmunka Group-Publishing-Foundation for his contribution to the case study with an interview. The author would also like to thank the key account manager Chris Kinsey and the client services manager Andrea Mansell from Lightning Source Inc. in Milton Keynes, UK for accepting the author in a meeting and conducting the interviews. They gave valuable insights about the printing and publishing industry.

The author is also grateful to the flat mates, Ali Tarik Tecer and Cathal McCann for their help and Evren Başbuğ for the cover design.

The Future Of Supply Chain Outsourcing?

Finally, the author likes to dedicate this research to his father Mehmet Nuri Kutlu, his mother Gülberk Kutlu and his sister Gül Kutlu who supported him with their unconditional love.

Foreword

The battle for leadership has shifted from company versus company to one company's supply chain versus another's. Competition is no longer between companies but between supply chains. Supply chain management is one of the most crucial aspects of business for competitive advantage. Although 4PL is a relatively new concept for supply chain outsourcing, it is growing fast. 4PL vendors bring together and centrally manage the complete supply chain for a company or a specific industry. The aims of this research were to analyse the reasons for utilising 4PL and investigate how 4PL vendors meet clients' requirements. Four elements were identified in the framework: Motives for utilising 4PL, relationship management and strategic development, 4PL models, supplier- client selection and drawbacks and risks of utilising 4PL. The topic was evaluated around these four elements to answer the research questions. A case study of the printing and publishing industry containing interviews with all parties in the relationship shed light on the issues from every angle related to 4PL outsourcing to compare and contrast theory and practice. The key points for competitive advantage were understanding, technology integration, compatibility, delivering and integration of stock. However, contrary to the literature, high cost of utilising 4PL did not seem to exist for the client in this particular case study.

The Future Of Supply Chain Outsourcing?

About this Book

This book is for those who are looking to know all about Fourth Party Logistics (4PL).

This book is produced using 4PL methods, printed in print runs of one plus books in three global centers and delivered directly or indirectly throughout the supply chain.

Describing 4PL is like describing the offside rule. However, once you understand the principles it really is simple. You can then understand why some corporate companies become lean companies just holding IPR and Trademarks, with very little in turnover, however high GP and NP along with exceptional earnings per head compared to the industry Key Performance Indicators (KPI).

This is an educational and practical book that starts to address how 4PL can change your business. There are a number of other books out there that are too sterile in their approach. The author approached 80 consulting companies only one would put its head up to be counted.

This book will reveal to you the, who, why and where and without doubt get every Finance Director within different companies asking if they can use 4PL. The book covers the client, the outsource provider and the

The Future Of Supply Chain Outsourcing?

consultancy company that sold the solution and made it work. 'Fourth Party Logistics' is less of a case study and more of a real practical business guide. The consultancy company in the book was the only one to put their experience to the test.

Şerafettin Kutlu has much to bring to the party and really does know his stuff.

He like very few others understands the number of internal and external factors that affect the 4PL process. Stake holders, employees, customers and suppliers need to buy-in to the working model. This working model needs to be not only a living model, but a functional document.

Within this book you will see how the industrial KPI of 18 months lead time has been reduced to 3 weeks. How a stock holding KPI is NIL STOCK, and that the TCO is much higher than traditional KPI's, however the cash flow and P&L is in better health because of this.

KPI of delivery are reduced from 5 days to 2 days, in some cases 24 hours! **Yes product is made to order**.

The whole existence of this humble publishing company challenges the larger publishing companies. The investment per book titles is $1,000^{th}$ of the normal KPI, diversity is embraced with 100+ new books brought on line within 3 months and break even of these new books within 9 months. These results are far

Fourth Party Logistics

better than the industry KPI, of larger publishing houses.

With a reduced overhead, 4PL allows companies to have not only a lower breakeven but a better focus on the core activity.

The downside on 4PL is that of cost, 4PL is not for the faint hearted, there is a steep learning curve. Rather than selling a solution that does not fit, VP Group offers an effective solution. Be warned however that 80% of the time the company, board or managers will hold back such change, therefore 4PL is doomed before it starts.

4PL can halt the decline of a company and hold a trade name for longer, or Last Man standing.

Many think 3PL is the same as 4PL. The difference is best explained as a 3PL provider will deliver your books, while a 4PL provider not only delivers books but prints them and bills the customer.

Implementation takes between 3 months and 5 years, thereafter the process is only as good as the relationship between provider and client. This is true of the setting up of a contract, where there is distrust this leads to non performance.

I, an example not covered by this book, however using the same principles. Production was moved to 4

The Future Of Supply Chain Outsourcing?

factories in 2 countries. The 4PL provision included cross boarder finance for the 4PL supplier and their suppliers with 3 European banks.

With 4PL it is hard to go back, using a consultant MIGHT be a good idea, but is not always, normal buying practise do not fit, if it's cheaper it might not be better. Moving all at once is not always the best idea either.

There are very few that understand 4PL once you have read this book, your mind will be focused.

Andrew Latchford
COO, VP Group

Table of contents

The Future Of Supply Chain Outsourcing?

Chapter 1: Introduction

1.0 Chapter Introduction

In this chapter, the definition of the topic, a brief background, the research aim, objectives, research questions, proposed research methodology and the structure of the book will be presented. The definition and background of 4PL along with the research aim, objectives and research questions will be the base for the development of this research.

1.1 Definition and Background of 4PL Outsourcing
1.1.1 Definition

"4PL's bring together and centrally manage the complete supply chain for a company or a specific industry, utilising best of breed 3PL's, technology service providers, supply chain specialists or consultants to provide a single supply chain solution that cannot be achieved by a 3PL alone. A 4PL is best described as an entity that positions itself between the manufacturer and the 3PL, managing the 3PL on behalf of the manufacturer, hence reducing the value of the 3PL to the supply chain" (BIG, 2004, p. 9).

1.1.2 Background

The definitions of logistics, supply chain management and outsourcing should be presented to provide a base

The Future Of Supply Chain Outsourcing?

for understanding 4PL outsourcing because these are crucial elements that establish the background for 4PL outsourcing.

In 1986, the Council of Logistics Management (CLM) defined logistics management as: *"The process of planning, implementing, and controlling the efficient, cost effective flow and storage of raw materials, in-process inventory, finished goods, and related information flow from point-of-origin to point-of-consumption for the purpose of conforming to customer requirements"* (Cooper *et al.*, 1997,p. 1). The important term in this definition is "information flow" because supply chain management evolved from the standpoint of information integrated material flow management. This emphasises a reduction in inventory within and across firms and clarifies the difference between more traditional approaches and integrated approaches across firm boundaries. The first appearance of the concept of supply chain management in the literature was in mid-1980s. It was simply defined as the integration of business processes across the supply chain. These business processes included activities like sourcing, procurement, warehousing, transportation, production scheduling, inventory management and customer service to move goods through to the customer. The evolution toward an integrated supply chain happened through embracing suppliers and customers. It embodied a change from product orientation to customer orientation and a change in the relationship between the parties from the adversarial attitude of conflict to one of mutual support and cooperation. A number of authors defined the objectives of supply chain management as synchronising the requirements of the customers with the flow of materials from suppliers by increasing customer service, reducing inventory investment and building competitive advantage and value (Cooper *et al.*, 1997). Supply chain management cited in Cooper *et al.*, (1997) was defined as the integration of business processes from end user through original suppliers that provide products, services and information that add value for customers by members of The International Centre for Competitive Excellence in 1994.

Outsourcing is defined as multiple supply chain management service provided by a single vendor on a contractual basis. Traditionally handled by the firms internally as support functions, activities such as transportation, distribution, warehousing, inventory management, order processing, and material handling have been given low priority compared with the other business functions. However, the need for developing sustainable competitive advantage, the growing emphasis on providing good customer service efficiently, and the strategic value of focusing on core businesses and re-engineering resulted in outsourcing those activities which was very different from traditional logistics. Outsourcing appears to be an important mechanism to realise the objective of increasing the quality of service and competitiveness despite some cost constraints. Globalisation of

The Future Of Supply Chain Outsourcing?

business, the continued growth in global markets, increasing demands on supply chain management, more complex supply chains and the increasing popularity of just in time (JIT) principles are some of the factors that may act as driving forces behind outsourcing. Therefore, tailored and multi-dimensional services linking transportation, warehousing, inventory management and others are keys for adding value through superior and speedy customer service (Razzaque and Sheng, 1998).

Public warehousing may be the oldest form of outsourcing in logistics according to Goldsmith (1989) cited in Razzaque and Sheng (1998). Then marketing, packaging, transportation, distribution, import and export were added to the list. After that, third party providers are being utilised for value-added activities. However, the list is expanding. Third party providers are often asset-based vendors, which offer physical logistics services primarily through the use of their own assets, typically a truck fleet or group of warehouses or both (Razzaque and Sheng, 1998). In the last and present wave, there is the 4PL vendor, which is management and consultancy based and creates a supply chain network between suppliers and clients chain by contracting other vendors on for the entire supply chain management (Hertz and Alfredsson, 2003).

1.2 Research Aim, Objectives and Research Questions

1.2.1 Research Aim

- To analyse the reasons for utilising 4PL and investigate how 4PL vendors meet clients' requirements.

1.2.2 Research Objectives

- To analyse the core competencies of 4PL vendors.
- To identify the pros and cons of utilising 4PL.
- To analyse important aspects of 4PL type relationships.
- To analyse the role of the physical service provider in the relationship.
- To conduct a literature review to reveal the key issues in 4PL.
- To identify and conduct a suitable case study to reflect 4PL practice.

1.2.3 Research Questions

- How do 4PL vendors meet the growing complexity of expectations and demands?
- Why do clients utilise 4PL?

1.3 Proposed Research Methodology

The proposed research methodology for this research will be a case study in the printing and publishing industry, which will be generated with the findings of four interviews. A case study was decided to be the most appropriate methodology for this research due to the types of research questions. A total of four interviews will be made with all parties in the relationship in order to evaluate the theoretical framework from every angle. The data will then be analysed utilising pattern matching.

The pattern matching data is found at the back of the book in appendices 5.

1.4 Structure

In Chapter 1, definition of 4PL outsourcing, a background, the research aim, objectives, the research questions, and proposed research methodology was presented.

Chapter 2, Literature review will start off with an introduction and carry on with the elements of the theoretical framework as titles. Motives for utilising 4PL, relationship management and strategic development, 4PL models, supplier-client selection will be presented with various references from academic journals, books and figures. Finally, it will conclude with drawbacks and risks of utilising 4PL.

In Chapter 3, Research methodology, research paradigms, methodologies, case study design, case study types, case study selection, data collection methods, interviews and interview question design and data analysis methods will be presented. The pattern matching table should be seen as the data analysis method in the appendices along with the interview questions.

In Chapter 4, the elements of the theoretical framework will be evaluated with case study findings separately for each party that took part in the interviews. The findings will then be compared and contrasted in the chapter summary.

In Chapter 5, case study findings will be discussed separately with each element of the theoretical framework. This will enable the reader to see whether there are any similarities or differences between what was mentioned in the literature review and what was discovered after the case study. The discussion will then be summarised in the chapter summary.

Chapter 6 will consist of conclusions and recommendations. The conclusions will enable the reader to see whether the research aim and objectives were achieved. The research questions will also be answered briefly. The chapter will then conclude with operational recommendations and recommendations for further research. Appendices and references will be presented as final sections of this research dissertation.

Chapter 2: Literature Review

2.0 Chapter Introduction

Fourth party logistics is a relatively new concept in supply chain outsourcing and very little research has been done on it. Seven motives are identified for its utilisation and they will be reviewed in the section called "motives for utilising 4PL". These motives will establish a critical evaluation of why 4PL is utilised. A number of references from different authors and academics will be given to compare and contrast different ideas. Some figures will also be used, to help the demonstration of theory related to 4PL.

"Relationship management and strategic development" section will follow "motives for utilising 4PL". Relationships are very important in the business world, especially in outsourcing, because companies work together to achieve goals. In this section 4PL type of relationships in particular will be analysed. Thus, each party's perceptions will be revealed. 4PL models and supplier- client selection will be discussed in the following section. The decision about how to outsource, rather than why to outsource supply chain management functions will be analysed. Some selection models are highlighted in the literature and they will be evaluated in detail. This element will also be evaluated from the 4PL vendor's side as well as the client's because they both are active parties in selection.

The Future Of Supply Chain Outsourcing?

There are not always the pros in business world, and utilising 4PL might not always be the best solution for a company. Therefore, the pros should outweigh the cons to get the best out of utilising 4PL. Otherwise, it is not logical to utilise it in the first place. Thus, the next section will analyse the drawbacks and risks of utilising 4PL, considering issues such as implementation, business cultures, costs and operational risks. The theoretical framework will consist of a table along with a text to understand the elements of the framework and create a better picture in the reader's mind about how the concept works. The chapter will conclude with the chapter summary.

2.1 Motives For Utilising 4PL
2.1.1 Cost Reduction
Leading companies view supply chain excellence as a source of competitive advantage, profit generation, asset utilization, and cost reduction. In fact, traditional outsourcing agreements tend to focus only on operating cost reduction and asset transfer. However, a 4PL vendor has the primary responsibility for supply chain performance as a centralised point of contact with the client and approaches the supply chain integration through increased revenue, operating cost reduction, working capital reduction and fixed capital reduction. The most likely source of enhancements in performance come through the synchronisation of supply chain planning and execution activities across the supply chain participants and increased collaboration between independent supply chain participants (Bade and Mueller, 1999).

4PL vendors aligned with a host of 3PL providers can reduce costs and improve customer service by allowing companies to concentrate on their core competencies (Vaidyanathan, 2005). Moreover, the decision to go with a 3PL provider is usually based on cost; companies outsource non-core logistics activities to save money. However in 4PL, the company can take things a step further, and look at the supply chain with the customer and redesign it to make it more efficient (Tierney, 2004a).

4PL vendors need to emphasise their value proposition

to differentiate themselves from traditional 3PLs and make a quantum leap from providing basic third party logistics services to being a centralised point of contact for the customer with the responsibility of monitoring supply chain performance and solid cost reductions. However, the fixed costs of 4PL are high and affect product pricing. These high investments, which are required, remain as significant financial barriers for 4PL relationships. This leaves the company with the trade off between tying up some significant assets in an in-house operation or working with a vendor (Menzefricke, 2004).

One of the key promises of 4PL is visibility across multiple levels of the supply chain that buys time, options, and better fulfilment rates for customers. By visibility, companies can avoid such costly manoeuvres like hiring a second carrier to expedite an order, or buying a duplicate component at a higher price, only to end up with two identical components arriving at the same time in the same location. They can take the appropriate corrective action, which translates directly to lower costs, quicker time to market and faster revenues (Schwartz, 2003). Schwartz (2003) also states that customers should sign gain share agreements to save a set percentage of current costs that agree to forfeit some proportional amount if that percentage is not met. On the other hand, the 4PL vendor earns a higher fee, provided the savings are greater. Sharing the risks and rewards make sure that the 4PL vendor puts the most possible effort to get the job done. However, companies should think twice before giving total control to a 4PL vendor, because the ultimate responsibility for getting the job done still resides within the enterprise.

However, a pulp and paper industry survey cited in Trecha (2002) stated that most firms did not understand or consider the potential cost reductions of gain-sharing agreements as part of a continuous improvement initiative. According to the survey, buyers and sellers agreed that an additional 4% to more than 15% price/cost reduction still existed. Traditional practices impede customer service improvements as well as cost reduction and asset reliability advancements. Most traditional practices focus on short- term relationships, which take short term cost reductions into account. The survey showed that companies were stuck in the traditional push on price rather than total cost reduction due to lack of fundamental total cost measures and the inability to validate potential cost savings.

Moreover, other issues such as enterprise resource planning systems, day-to-day emergencies created by customer demands and shifting production schedules, also delayed supply chain advancement. Studies have shown that firms have achieved only 40 to 70% of what was actually available, leaving another 30 to 60% of available improvements (Trecha 2002). However, an Accenture survey showed that cost reduction was only the initial outcome of supply chain outsourcing. While cost reductions and savings were significant drivers of supply chain outsourcing, a broader view of the benefits to be gained should be taken into account. Although increased profitability tops the list in the survey, significant numbers of respondents also cited other desirable business outcomes. Figure 2.1 shows that 74% of the respondents reported that they measure and manage outsourcing performance by looking at a range of broad business outcomes (Accenture, 2004).

Improved profitability
64%
Improved management
focus 39%
Speed to market 37%
Increased revenue 33%
Increased customer loyalty
25%
Market share 23%

Figure 2.1 Business outcome metrics companies use to measure outsourcing performance
Base: Respondents reporting using business outcomes; 418 individuals or 74% of all respondents

2.1.2 Adding Value

Since the appearance of 4PL providers in the late 1990s, globalisation and the increased complexity of the supply chain have changed the ways in which companies were working together. Manufacturers' and retailers' continuous growth through acquisitions, mergers, and alliances often result in disparate supply chains existing across a single multinational corporation. This is where the 4PL vendors step in: They provide value added services through coordination and communication across different service providers, geographies, time zones, and business units. However, 4PLs might have a hard time in positioning themselves within the supply chain due to their wide- ranging origins. Some are equipped with the management expertise required to supervise the entire transportation network across multi modes, geographies, and industries, but rely on their 3PL partners to deliver the practical element. Others have the practical capabilities without the consultancy knowledge. Whatever their origins, the real differentiator is the ability to offer value added services that suit customers' requirements (Love, 2004).

3PL providers traditionally offer standard warehousing and transportation. Their offerings appeal to a larger number of customers with basic needs. 4PL vendors deal with more complex and consultative solutions for every individual client. They add value to standard services in terms of technological expertise, higher levels of adaptation and customised solutions.

The Future Of Supply Chain Outsourcing?

However, they might use 3PL providers for standard services (Hertz and Alfredsson, 2003). 4PL providers differentiate themselves from traditional service providers by offering expanded services with higher value added and creating market approaches, which use information integration across the whole supply chain (Van Hoek and Chong, 2001).

The 4PL value proposition is like a chain reaction achieved through revenue growth, operating cost reduction, working capital reduction, and fixed capital reduction. All of these come together and result in increased profitability, reduced capital investment and finally greater shareholder value as shown in Figure 2.2 (Foster, 1999a).

Figure 2.2: The 4PL Value Proposition, (Foster, 1999a, p.62)

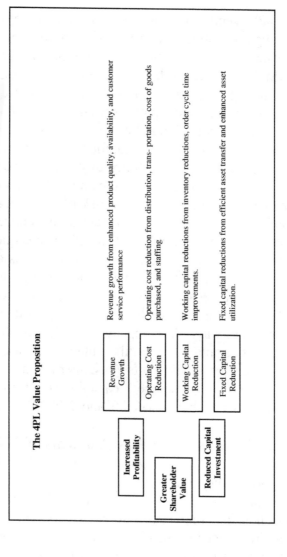

The 4PL Value Proposition

Increased Profitability	Revenue Growth	Revenue growth from enhanced product quality, availability, and customer service performance
	Operating Cost Reduction	Operating cost reduction from distribution, trans-portation, cost of goods purchased, and staffing
Greater Shareholder Value		
	Working Capital Reduction	Working capital reductions from inventory reductions, order cycle time improvements.
Reduced Capital Investment	Fixed Capital Reduction	Fixed capital reductions from efficient asset transfer and enhanced asset utilization.

The Future Of Supply Chain Outsourcing?

A 4PL vendor can deliver comprehensive solutions through its ability to affect the entire supply chain (Foster, 1999a). On the other hand, the company Frost & Sullivan believes that 4PL is not the next logical step for all logistics service providers, because a candidate organisation needs to have very strong capabilities such as strategy consulting, business process review, and redesign, technology integration and savvy people management with the ability to combine and manage the best of breed skills of companies. This can be a real challenge for vendors, as the risk of not being able to implement the value chain across the entire supply chain will cause problems. Therefore, the question is whether 4PL is the right move or not. 4PL is all about working with others, and maintaining a sound relationship because a single company trying to act as a 4PL integrator will not have all the capabilities needed along the way. A company considering 4PL as a business option should internally assess its competencies against its customer's and then be prepared to insource capabilities from other organisations where needed (Cabodi, 2004).

2.1.3 Removal of the Key Problems of 3PL

Logistics 15-20 years ago were cash cow services, but nowadays they are very efficient and lean. Most 3PL providers have grown out of transportation or warehousing companies that are asset based. This is the key difference between 3PLs and 4PLs. The former has its own warehousing network and fleet of trucks whereas the latter has no assets. This might be

Fourth Party Logistics

considered as a strength for 3PL providers, but is also their weakness. Their aim is to keep trucks full, but on the other hand 4PL vendors' aim is to optimise 3PL's assets. The customer bargaining power is so high that logistics companies are running on low margins and it is likely that 3PL providers are being driven under. In 4PL, the vendor has the perspective of a broad view of the supply chain. Customers demand integration and more intelligent solutions. Most 3PLs cannot provide them (Jones, 2001). Although 4PL vendors admit that 3PLs have superior expertise in warehousing and transportation, they argue that these operational tasks only provide one-time reductions. According to 4PL vendors, 3PL providers cannot deliver ongoing savings and efficiencies because they lack the optimal combination of technology, transportation service, and warehousing capabilities.

Moreover, a 4PL vendor is free to find the best breed in each category. Large companies frequently hire consultants to review proposals from 3PLs, handle bids, select vendors, and align business processes with supply chain plans to put the best breed together. Then the question becomes: Who needs to be in control of the supply chain, and who can manage it better. After all, the 3PL provider should know its own suppliers' and customers' business needs better. Therefore, it has to run the supply chain. Yet in truth, the answer is not that easy, and apparently 3PLs have not really made sizable improvements in customer service and profitability (Foster, 1999b).

The Future Of Supply Chain Outsourcing?

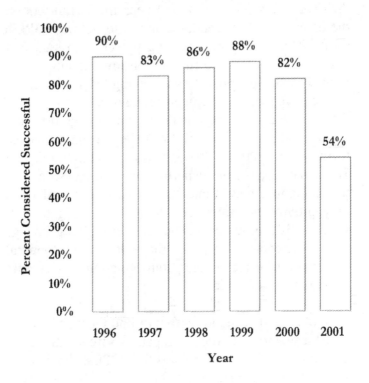

Figure 2.3: 3PL Outsourcing Success Ratio, (BIG, 2004, p.5)

As shown in Figure 2.3, the 3PL providers had a promising success ratio of 90% in 1996, but could not sustain this level of success. There was a huge drop in success ratio in 2001 from previous years. This drop was mainly due to growing demands of clients and the lack of realisation of service level commitments. 3PL providers could not customise their offerings and lacked consultative, knowledge-based skills. Their strategic management skills were not efficient enough to keep control over the whole supply chain. Therefore, the concept of 4PL was introduced to meet the expectations and better match demands (BIG, 2004).

A 1994 Andersen Consulting survey of 250 organisations in the UK found that two-thirds of respondents actually felt that their initial expectations of 3PLs were not being met. While many 3PL providers could deliver warehousing, transportation and fleet management services, few were able to cover the full range of supply chain requirements that included services such as logistics IT development and order processing. This shortfall in service means that the organisation needs to assemble a combination of outsourced and in-house service components to manage its supply chain effectively. Therefore, a management team is required to spend a disproportionate amount of time managing the relationships and resources to make 3PL work. The performance of the overall supply chain inevitably fails to keep pace with global best practice levels and does not have the capacity to eliminate inefficiencies in all aspects through process reengineering (Gattorna, 1998).

2.1.4 Efficient Information Flow

Information has always been one of the most important elements of the distribution process. Order communications were seen as a major component in the management of performance within physical distribution channels. Towards the end of the 1980s, information became one of the most important points for competitive advantage. The core value offered by 4PL vendors is in managing the flow of information between outsourced supply chain partners and the companies. Management planning and control is gained through efficient and timely information flow. The role of information management is crucial in the development of supply chain strategy and operational issues. The broadest application of information technology EDI (electronic data interchange) offers advantages such as an ability to offer control over the movements, thereby enhancing the ability to participate in JIT (just-in-time), and ECR (efficient consumer response). Information flow also reduces labour costs and content, as well as the routine tasks that are typical sources for error (Gattorna and Walters, 1996).

4PL vendors are highly information based and they coordinate multiple asset-based players on behalf of their clients. They tend to participate much more in supply chain coordination rather than supply chain operational services, which implies a great focus on using information for competitive advantage. Using IT tools effectively also enables vendors to create and manage an e-supply chain infrastructure to leverage supply chain competencies. Findings indicate that IT tools support the expansion and customisation of logistics service offerings. However ensuring efficient information flow is, by no means an easy task. Strategic and supply chain wide benefits will not be realised if approaches to the flow of information remain fragmented (Van Hoek and Chong, 2001).

Any item of information, which is not, managed properly- by not being synchronised with the corresponding goods movement or with other items of information or by being inaccurate- results in customer dissatisfaction. Responding to customer demand is not possible without proper management of the information flow. Information on any factor also affects forecasting, which is very important for operational and financial performance of the supply chain. The performance indicators include total supplier lead times, supply chain costs, customer satisfaction levels and forecast accuracy. Information, which can affect the current forecasts, needs to be shared immediately with the parties upstream. Supply chain integration is achieved by combining goods movement with the flow of operational and financial information between parties. Therefore, information flow is also crucial for inventory management and monitoring of goods movement. The most important thing is being able to utilise the information, because information is unimportant unless it can be utilised by the 4PL vendor (Singh, 1996).

The Future Of Supply Chain Outsourcing?

Another tool for information flow is the Internet. The Internet can provide the flow of information crucial for SCM, either in the form of Web pages accessible only to specific vendors or by means of an intranet. When the manufacturer is dependent on vendors to maintain sufficient inventories, it must inform the vendor not only of its upcoming needs; but also needs to give access to current inventory levels. 4PLs act as an interface and a single point of contact between the parties. In many industries, the supply chain represents roughly 75 percent of the operating expenses, and the Internet utilisation has the advantages of speed, decreased cost, flexibility along with the potential of shortening the supply chain. The Internet allows instant transfer of information, which helps firms keep pace with their environments. Internet based e-procurement reduces costs by decreasing the use of paper and labour and by providing better tracking. Although utilising the Internet requires an enormous amount of trust and implementation cost, it pays back eventually with an e-synchronised supply chain (Lankford, 2004).

2.1.5 Change Management and Collaboration

Logistics practiced between the mid-1960s and mid-1990s evolved from a traditional focus on purchasing to a broader and more integrated emphasis on value creation in the new millennium. Effective collaboration and change management within chain entities are essential to achieve goals, individually and collectively. The crucial point is crystallising when collaboration is useful, what to change, what to change to and how to make changes happen (Kampstra *et al.*, 2006). A survey conducted by Supply Chain Management Review and Computer Science Corporation cited in Kampstra *et al.*, (2006) showed that 44 percent of the organisations had functions for supplier and customer collaboration. However, only about 35 percent of the collaboration initiatives turned out to be successful. It was due to lack of genuine desire to collaborate among parties.

One of the approaches to maintain supply chain collaboration is utilising a fourth party logistics (4PL) entity as a centralised "optimisation tool" to coordinate and control the channel. The collaboration leader either chooses to coordinate the collaboration itself or it appoints another entity to be the coordinator. A supply chain member or a non-member (4PL) is chosen. Regardless of collaboration type, at some point in the collaboration, the group will face a supply chain constraint that limits further collaboration. A 4PL type of collaboration is most likely to have policy constraint, which basically involves removing the old rules and

The Future Of Supply Chain Outsourcing?

introducing new ones that are consistent with the supply chain strategy. These constraints are intangible thus, difficult to identify for management. Changing the policies and the cultural mindset of employees is tough and may take years. It is very important to implement sound change management and collaboration on the basis of agreeing on how to distinguish an offer from competitive chains in the chosen market segment (Kampstra *et al.*, 2006). On the other hand, Kerr (2006) states that some providers are starting to develop frameworks that allow them to track trade-offs between scale and specialised expertise, which focus on why to implement change management, what influences those decisions rather than how. The goal is to determine whether there are potential benefits of economies of scale. Consultancies step in where shippers lack the expertise to build such frameworks to define the scope of worldwide logistics activities and determine the appropriate balance of activities among regions (Kerr, 2006).

Supply chain managers need to be change managers-not just managing change within the organisation but also managing the way of relationships between organisations. One of the ways to achieve this coordination is by utilising a 4PL service provider. 4PLs make sure more agile response is achieved even in complex networks. As a pipeline integrator, 4PLs make use of their expertise and knowledge of managing global supply chains (Christopher and Towill, 2001).

2.1.6 Leanness and Agility

Naylor *et al.*, (1999, p.107) provide a useful definition of the two paradigms as follows: *"Agility means using market knowledge and a virtual corporation to exploit profitable opportunities in a volatile marketplace. Leanness means developing a value stream to eliminate all waste including time, and to ensure a level schedule."*

Christopher (2000) argues that lean concepts work well where demand is relatively stable and predictable and product variety is low. However, there are many other markets, where availability is the key. This leads to the emergence of "quick response" which is the key point of the agile paradigm. A higher level of agility is required where demand is volatile and the customer requirement for variety is high. Nevertheless, "lean" and "agile" are not mutually exclusive paradigms and may be married to advantage in a number of ways. Being truly competitive requires not just the appropriate manufacturing strategy, but rather an appropriate holistic supply chain strategy.

In particular, the elimination of muda (waste) and level scheduling successfully deliver a wide range of products to those markets where cost is the primary order winning criterion. The lean paradigm best works, when the winning criterion is cost. However, agility becomes crucial, when service and customer value enhancement are primary requirements for market winning. Lead-time needs to be reduced in lean manufacturing. The difference between leanness and agility is the service level (availability) in terms of the total value provided to the customer (Aitken *et al.*, 2002).

There are a few practical ways of marrying leanness and agility due to a number of common elements between the two.

The Pareto curve approach: Pareto's rule, which states that 80 percent of the volume is generated from just 20 percent of the total product lines, applies. This 20 percent should be managed in a different way than the remaining 80 percent are managed. As shown in Figure 2.4, 20 percent of products by volume are likely to be more predictable and hence lend themselves to lean principles, whereas the slow moving 80 percent are less predictable and require an agile mode of management (Harris, 2004).

Fourth Party Logistics

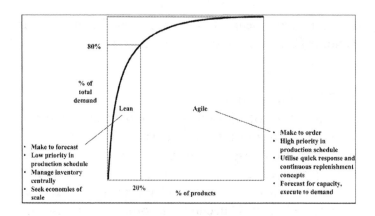

Figure 2.4: The Pareto distribution, (Christopher and Towill, 2001, p.240)

The de-coupling approach: This marrying of the paradigms is achieved through the creation of a "de-coupling point" using what may be termed as strategic inventory. The idea is to hold inventory in some generic or modular form and only complete the final assembly when the precise customer requirement is known. This concept of postponement is achieved by lean methods up to the de-coupling point and agile methods beyond it (Jones and Towill, 1999).

Separation of "base" and "surge" demands: Base demand can be forecast on the basis of past history, which can be met through lean methods. However, surge demand is provided through more flexible and probably higher cost methods. Strategies being employed in the fashion industry where the base demand is sourced in low cost countries and the surge

41

demand locally nearer to the market can be given as an example (Christopher and Towill, 2001).

2.1.7 E-supply chain

Development of information and communication technologies has resulted in e-business to be one of the most important aspects of SCM. Various new and existing players started responding with their own Web sites and electronic marketing channels. The creation of e-supply chains is needed, in order to realise the promise of e-business and earn back investments. E-supply chains provide base level operational performance in the physical sphere (fulfillment, etc.), as well as a backbone to help realise more advanced e-business applications. Problems such as stock shortfalls, irregularities and unpredictability in order quantities in the chain (Forrester effect), occur due to the complexities of trading in volatile markets (Lee *et al.*, 1997).

Therefore, utilisation of relevant practices and efficient information flow are crucial. However, the question then becomes: Why do information based companies achieve such poor supply chain performance. It is due to poor management solutions rather than technology. The two basic problems are having a partial, as opposed to an integral approach and having an operational approach, as opposed to a strategic approach (Van Hoek, 2001). Figure 2.5 illustrates primary dimensions to assess supply chain approach to e- business.

Fourth Party Logistics

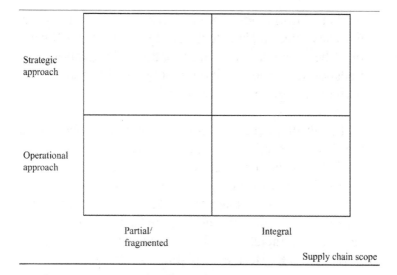

Figure 2.5: Supply chain approaches to e-business
(Van Hoek, 2001, p.24)

The true e-supply chain needs to be in the upper right quadrant. Connectivity between supply chain layers is implemented as a strategic approach in the upper right quadrant. Information flow is not only used for transactional purposes but also for strategic advantage. Information integration by 4PL vendors leverages operational information for the strategic benefits of learning, supply chain engineering and competitive differentiation. The operational information is recorded and can be used to monitor transportation links, identify opportunities for lowering costs by shifting volumes between routes or realising a competitive advantage through differentiating services in response to the

The Future Of Supply Chain Outsourcing?

market information (Van Hoek, 2001). However, Crowley cited in Van Hoek (2001) argues that 4PLs are in the center of information integration of transportation and distribution only and thus represent a partially integrated supply chain scope.

Although there are promising integration opportunities via Web- based or e- supply chains, creation and implementation of integrated supply chains is often overlooked because they require tremendous resources, a great deal of management time and energy, large organisation-wide changes, huge commitment from suppliers/partners, and sophisticated technical infrastructure. Besides, off-the- shelf supply chain software solutions are not suitable for every firm; because different supply chains have different requirements. Therefore, firms need to have the expertise to understand their particular needs to match the most suitable solution among a number of available solutions. They need to pick the one they can successfully implement or customise according to their requirements (Pant *et al.*, 2003). *"A survey conducted in 2000 revealed that while 64 percent of companies have an electronic business strategy and 35 percent claim to have a Web-enabled supply chain, only four percent actually have an electronic supply chain management system. Furthermore 62 percent of respondents do not see the acquisition of electronic business technology by their competitors as a threat. The main findings also revealed that the greatest restriction to optimizing electronic business capability within the organization was lack of understanding"* (Article, 2000, p10).

2.2 Relationship Management and Strategic Development

As an intermediary between the client and the physical service provider, one of the main challenges for a 4PL vendor is to balance an ability of adaptation and standardisation. The way this is balanced has vital importance on resources needed, activities to be performed and on core competency development. A classification of providers is made in Figure 2.6 according to abilities of customer adaptation and general problem solving (Hertz and Alfredsson, 2003).

	Customer adaptation	
Problem solving ability	Relatively high	High
High	**Service Developer** Example: An advanced modular system of a large variety of services and a common IT- system used for all customers.	**Customer Developer** Example: The TPL firms develop advanced customer solutions for each customer. Enhancing of the knowledge in common. The role more of a consultant.
Relatively high	**Standard TPL Provider** Example: A highly standardised modular system where customers are offered their own relatively simple combination of standardised services.	**Customer Adapter** Example: Totally dedicated solutions involving basic services for each customer. TPL firm is seen as a part of the customer organisation.

Figure 2.6: TPL firms classified according to abilities of general problem solving and customer adaptation (Hertz and Alfredsson, 2003, p.141).

Fourth Party Logistics

4PL relationships fit into the customer developer type of relationships in the upper right quadrant in Figure 2.6, which involve a high integration with the customer. These types of relationships are the most advanced and difficult, often in the form of taking over the whole supply chain operations of the client. They tend to be long term and involve sharing risks and awards. The relationships develop over time due to increasing volumes and types of activities. As the relationships develop, so do the suppliers. Suppliers evaluate their skills and competencies necessary to increase customer adaptation and general problem solving as a result of gradual developing. An increased degree of integration results in a higher level of commitment and stronger implications (Hertz and Alfredsson, 2003). As the Accenture 2004 survey confirmed: Supply chain management outsourcing is more than just a contract, it is a relationship. It is not enough to sign up and hand off. Effective outsourcing requires active involvement from both parties. Most of the participants in the survey stated that they were satisfied from the initial achievements in the first year and much more satisfied as the relationship went along over years (Accenture, 2004).

Adaptation is an important point in supply chain outsourcing, because nowadays nobody runs their supply chain in the same way and each has a different way of dealing with operations. That is why standardisation is not fully evolved. Another vital aspect of 4PL relationships is "trust" due to sharing of risks and rewards. Suppliers need to treat clients' business just like their own because there is much at stake (Schwartz, 2003).

Another survey revealed that advanced service requirements, shared risk-reward arrangements, global expansion pressures and demand for broader expertise were primary drivers behind 4PL relationships (Biederman, 2005). *"57 percent of respondents said that existing 3PLs were best suited to provide 4PL services, 25 percent said consultants and 22 percent cited technology companies. Twelve percent of those surveyed currently use a 4PL model, and survey findings indicate the model will continue to prosper"* (Biederman, 2005, p.29).

2.3 4PL Models and Supplier- Client Selection

Pressing logistics decisions are about how to outsource and what influences these decisions rather than why. If one global vendor cannot provide every logistics need, is there an ideal mix of contract and in-house resources. There are some key points to bear in mind. For instance, the supply chain for inbound raw materials or low volume outbound products have different requirements. Identical components shipped to aftermarket delivery centers have wider delivery windows than loads of containers of electronic components arriving at an assembly plant. Therefore, the mix will be different for each market and company. Each company should have unique logistics resources. Moreover, they should have the internal skills to select and evaluate vendors. They should be able to make the difficult decision of whether to hand off logistics services to a vendor (Kerr, 2006).

Although logistics outsourcing has been utilised for many years, it couldn't go further than transportation and warehousing (Hertz and Alfredsson, 2003). Over the past few years though, providers have built up capabilities to go beyond the traditional vertical relationship and develop horizontal relationships. That's how the 4PL concept has emerged (Jharkharia and Shankar 2007).

Jharkharia and Shankar (2007) present a methodology

for the selection of a logistics service provider that consists of preliminary screening of the available providers via analytic network process (ANP)- based final selection. They state that one of the most important key points of selection is identifying what is needed from the provider. Many providers are offering a variety of services and the criteria for the selection are complex. Therefore, the selection of the appropriate provider is a difficult task as the number of selection criteria increases. For the development of an ANP model; Jharkharia and Shankar (2007) identify four major criteria named as compatibility, cost, quality and reputation, which are supported by four sub-criteria.

There are also enablers that support sub-criteria. First of all, a team of competitive managers should be developed to undertake change management. The team should include members from various functional areas. Secondly, the expectations and objectives from outsourcing should be clearly identified to make sure there are fewer surprises. The user should specify nature of its business, requirements and orders before the evaluation of potential providers. Finally, ANP-based methodology is recommended for the final selection of a provider. ANP- based methodology is concluded through comparison and evaluation of major criteria, sub-criteria and enablers.

However, Andersson and Norrman (2002) state that there are various problems related to the application of the model and supplier selection. These problems include accepting the information given by the prospective suppliers as genuine, which may not always be. Comparison might be a tough task because different suppliers have different solutions, which are not always comparable. Therefore, the selection process might take months considering all of these issues.

Just like a client needs to evaluate potential suppliers, suppliers need to decide whether there is a viable opportunity to serve the requirements and expectations of potential clients. The supplier also needs to know the problems, inefficiencies and needed improvements in a potential client's supply chain to address them in the most efficient way. The supplier's capabilities should match desired outcomes from the relationship. A lot of relationships fail due to the lack of communication and misunderstandings between parties. Therefore, the gap between what clients receive and what they expect to receive should be minimised. There are some diagnostic tools to help suppliers customise their solutions for each client. Most of them are quantitative tools that rely on performance measures and benchmarking techniques. Some organisations also offer tools to undertake benchmarking analysis and value assessment models to help companies in the evaluation process of a potential client (Foggin *et al.,* 2004)

2.4 Drawbacks and Risks of Utilising 4PL

The emergence of 4PL happened due to the need for increased service levels and pressure on costs. But the important question is whether 3PL or 4PL is more suitable for a particular company. It is hard a question to answer because both of them have their own advantages and disadvantages. 3PL providers might have the internal controls to implement new technologies and plans, but on the other hand they cannot really deliver the required customer service levels and the profitability. There will certainly be more than one correct answer to this question, but it is likely that most 3PLs will turn over the function to a 4PL (Foster, 1999b).

Successful implementation of 4PL requires a clear understanding of establishment and operational risks. 4PL concept is a flexible model that can be adapted to include different partner organisations according to the industry structure, objectives and targets. Due to this flexibility, there is a risk that it may be difficult to convince a potential primary client to cooperate with one of its competitors to form a 4PL venture. Confidentiality issues between competing organisations may occur.

Therefore, firewall procedures must be in place to make sure clients cannot access any confidential information. Another risk is that 4PL relationships often are long-term partnerships. It is difficult to change partners because of high switching costs. The same risk applies even if a company is working with 3PL providers. Switching to another service arrangement not only includes penalty costs for breaking the long-term contract but also can result in an initial drop in efficiency. The new provider needs to grow accustomed to the clients operations and invest time to establish a good working relationship with the personnel (Gattorna, 1998).

Reed Carr, transportation development manager with chipmaker giant *Intel Corp.*, interviewed logistics pros that had used 4PLs and backed off when they didn't see the excepted results. He stated that some people swore at 4PL due to negative experiences. As a result, some companies like Selectron Corp., a provider of electronic manufacturing services, keep supply chain expertise in-house rather than utilising 4PL. James Molzon, Solectron's vice president of customer fulfillment and global logistics, stated that they were a 4PL vendor for their customers by managing a variety of third-party service providers to bring service. That was a way to eliminate loss of control, risks associated with long term relationships and disagreements over the interpretation of metrics (Richardson, 2005).

Changing industry dynamics may make obsolete some or all of the services that the 4PL organisation originally provides. An assessment for the long-term viability of the 4PL organisation for the clients and industries must be made through scenario planning. It should then be structured so that it is able to change the

The Future Of Supply Chain Outsourcing?

nature and mix of service providers to the venture as the nature of supply chain and industry also changes. There is also a risk of excessive disruption to the client's existing business once the contractual arrangements are established. These might include procedures to move client personnel into their new roles in the 4PL organisation. Therefore, a detailed transition plan must be developed up-front (Gattorna, 1998).

Dealing with the management aspect of the supply chain might be considered as a disadvantage for 4PLs, because the physical evidence is little and hard to measure. Some traditional companies might think that 4PL is only a concept for the sake of a concept; not a real opportunity (Love, 2004). Moreover, serious investment is required and some smaller companies might not be able to handle it. Even if they are able to handle it, they might not share the idea of 'gain and share' because of their culture and working habits. For instance, head of global accounts for the logistics division for UPS Logistics, Andreas Janetzko, states that the logistics directors he talks to, often react defensively to any mention of 4PL (Tierney, 2004b). *"They feel under threat at the thought of an outside organisation managing their overall logistics activities, applying intelligence and orchestrating everything that goes on. They feel that's their job"* (Tierney, 2004b, p.18).

Fourth Party Logistics

Diversity also, is a double-edged sword for 4PL vendors. It might be an advantage or a disadvantage. Overall mechanisms are so diverse that a model for a particular region doesn't fit another region. Diversity brings huge scope for 4PLs, but they need massive amount of knowledge for success (Roberts, 2003).

There are 4PL relationships that don't work considering all the risks and drawbacks of 4PL. However, in spite of all potential drawbacks, the number of companies utilising 4PL is growing. Handling the risks is all about making the right choices and arranging necessary change management activities (Onge, 2002).

2.5 Theoretical Framework

4PL Models, Supplier and Client Selection

Physical Service Provider (3PL)

Service provided by

Service provided for (client)

4PL vendor

CLIENT

Relationship Management and Strategic Development

- **Motives for utilising 4PL**
- **Drawbacks and risks of utilising 4PL**

Fourth Party Logistics

Theoretical Framework

The theoretical framework consists of three parties around the four elements, which are "relationship management and strategic development", "4PL models, supplier- client selection", "motives for utilising 4PL" and "drawbacks and risks of utilising 4PL". The 4PL vendor is placed between the client and the physical service provider. 4PL relationships are quite complex particularly for the supplier and the client. The 4PL provider is the client of the 3PL provider. However, the 4PL vendor has its own client for which it provides the service through the 3PL provider. In other words, the 4PL vendor outsources the service from its supplier (3PL) and the client outsources the service from the 4PL vendor.

Moreover, the 4PL provider's client has clients of its own which are specified as final customers. However, the final customers will not be dealt with in the research. Unlike the other points in the framework, relationships between those parties affect all three parties in the framework. Certain questions will be asked to each cluster about their relationships between each other to highlight important aspects of the relationships. The issues are related with the 4PL vendor, as well as the other parties. The way that the issues apply for each cluster might vary. Therefore, the concept will be dealt with from each side of the relationship. Certain questions will be asked to the interviewees to understand different opinions about the same issue.

The Future Of Supply Chain Outsourcing?

Other elements, such as motives for utilising 4PL, drawbacks and risks of utilising 4PL, 4PL models, supplier- client selection; which are as important as the relationships, are mentioned in the framework. All these aspects that are in the framework are discussed in detail in the sections of the literature review. The interviews in the case study will reveal how 4PL vendors meet clients' requirements in terms of crucial points for providing the service, the reasons for utilising 4PL and important points in how the 3PL provider provides the actual physical service. The case study will provide substantial information about 4PL practice.

When all elements of the framework are evaluated together, they will provide a base for understanding the development of the entire 4PL service. The interview questions will provide explanations of how things function and why events occur shedding light on the research questions, objectives and the research aim.

2.6 Chapter Summary

Elements of the theoretical framework were analysed in detail in this chapter to provide a base for understanding the development of 4PL outsourcing in the literature. The literature on 4PL was relatively limited because it is a new concept in supply chain management outsourcing. Although, the literature on 4PL outsourcing was limited, a number of references were gathered to demonstrate the theoretical framework. Important aspects of 4PL outsourcing were covered to help analyse the subject further in the case study. The theory was also supported with various figures and survey findings to create a better picture in the reader's head. Finally, the literature review will enable the author to design the case study and discuss the findings of the case study with what was discovered in the literature.

Chapter 3 : Research Methodology

3.0 Chapter Introduction

In this chapter the issues and data that need to be researched to fulfil the research aim, objectives, and questions will be presented. It will state why certain data was collected and why it was relevant to the nature of the research. There will be a section about the theory of research paradigms and the reasons behind choosing the particular paradigm. The research paradigm undertaken is related with the research aim, objectives, and questions. Therefore, the nature of the research aim, objectives, and questions will lead to a specific paradigm selection and confirm its relevancy. Finally, the research paradigm will lead to the particular research methodology undertaken, which will be case study. There will be sections about case study types and the case study design. The main focus of the methodology chapter will be the case study because it will shed light on the issues related to 4PL practice. There will also be a section about selection criteria. One might encounter some problems of access while trying to find an organisation to conduct a case study. The problems encountered will be mentioned. The research methodology will be dealt with, mentioning what data will be collected, from where it will be collected, when it will be collected and how it will be collected. Data collection methods will be about the interviews and the interview question design, which will contribute to the theoretical framework. It will mention with whom and why the interviews will be done and what and why will be asked. The methodology chapter will conclude with the data analysis methods mentioning how the data will be analysed, which will be the utilisation of pattern matching.

3.1 Methodology
3.1.1 Research Paradigms and Methodology

As Yin (1994) states about case studies, cited in Perry (1998, p.786): *"The methodology usually investigates a contemporary phenomenon within its real-life context when the boundaries between phenomenon and context are not clearly evident"*.

A paradigm in the context of research is about how the research is conducted and it offers a framework comprising an accepted set of theories, methods and ways of defining data. There are two main research paradigms that can be labeled as positivist and phenomenological, which may also be stated as quantitative and qualitative respectively. In a positivist research, reality is objective and singular and the researcher is independent from that being researched. In a phenomenological research, reality is subjective, open to argument and the researcher interacts with that being researched. Positivists are concerned with any concepts used in the research that are physically measurable or are objective facts. Positivistic paradigm associates itself with natural sciences such as biology. However, phenomenologist's use research methods to obtain different perceptions about a situation or phenomena and the paradigm is concerned with understanding human behavior, focusing on the meaning rather than the measurement. Research methodologies used under the phenomenological approach are an array of interpretative techniques, which seek to describe and translate. Therefore, the research methodology undertaken will ultimately depend on the research paradigm and the nature of the research, which is phenomenological in this case (Collis and Hussey, 2003).

3.2 Case Study Design

Types of research questions identify the research methodology and are important in the design of the case study. A basic categorisation for the types of questions is the familiar series: "Who", "what", "where", "how" and "why" (Yin, 1994).

Strategy	Form of research question	Requires control over behavioral events?	Focuses on contemporary events?
Experiment	How, why	Yes	Yes
Survey	Who, what, where, how many, how much	No	Yes
Archival analysis	Who, what, where, how many, how much	No	Yes/ No
History	How, why	No	No
Case study	How, why	No	Yes

Figure 3.1: Relevant situations for different research strategies (Yin, 1994, p.6).

Either of two possibilities arises if the research questions focus mainly on "what" questions. Some types of "what" questions are exploratory and this type of question is a justifiable rationale for conducting an exploratory study. Therefore any type of the five research strategies can be used. However, some types of "what" questions are in a form of a "how many" or "how much" line of inquiry. Such outcomes are more likely to be identified by conducting survey or archival analysis. Similarly "who" and "where" questions are likely to favor survey or archival analysis. Such strategies are advantageous when the research goal is to describe a phenomenon or when it is possible to predict certain outcomes (Yin, 1994).

As stated in Figure 3.1, "how" and "why" questions are more explanatory and likely to favor case studies, histories and experiments because such questions deal with operational links needing to be traced over time, rather than mere incidents. The case study is preferred in examining contemporary events, when manipulation over relevant behaviors is not possible, unlike in experiments (Yin, 1994).

When the type of research paradigm, which is phenomenological in this research, and the research questions are considered; this research favors case study as the research methodology. The design of the research is an action plan for getting from here to there, where "here" may be defined as the initial set of questions to be answered and "there" is the set of conclusions. In this research, the most appropriate way of getting from "here" to "there" is a case study. A case study is lead by the research questions to achieve findings. However, the design should not only indicate what data are to be collected, but also what is to be done after the data have been collected. This is important to link the data to the propositions and identify the criteria for interpreting the findings. Pattern matching technique will be utilised to compare and contrast several pieces of information from the same case. Several pieces of information provided by the interviewees will be summarised to reach conclusions (Yin, 1994).

A complete case study should specify conditions for designing an investigation, collecting the pertinent data, analysing the data and reporting the findings. In terms of designs, the author mainly deals with the logic, whereby initial research questions can be subjected to empirical testing by deciding between single and multiple case studies, selecting the specific cases to be studied, developing a case study protocol, defining the relevant data collection and analysis strategies. The selection criteria should include criticality for the theory, topical relevance, feasibility and access. Another important aspect of case studies is that they are designed to examine and specify the operational chain of events leading to the relevant outcomes. The crucial steps in the design are to specify outcomes of concern, reference existing theories in enumerating "how" and "why" questions to explain outcomes.

A final consideration is to design valid and reliable case studies (Yin, 1993).

3.3 Case Study Types

On the contrary, Yin (2003) assumes that case study research can be qualitative as well as quantitative. In this research, the research methodology is case study and the research undertaken has the characteristics of phenomenological research. Case studies are used when the phenomenon under study is not readily distinguishable from its context. There are at least six different types of case studies, based on a 2x3 matrix.

First, case study research can be based on single or multiple case studies; second whether single or multiple, it can be exploratory, descriptive or explanatory. Exploratory case studies aim at defining the questions and hypotheses of a subsequent study or at determining the feasibility of the desired research procedures. Descriptive case studies present a complete description of a phenomenon within its context. Explanatory case studies present data bearing on cause-effect relationships- explaining how events happened (Yin, 2003).

Case studies are appropriate when one is trying to analyse relationships and not just wanting to describe a situation. The major rationale is to cover both a particular phenomenon and its context, either because the context contains important explanatory variables about the phenomenon or the boundaries between context and phenomenon are not clearly evident. The nature of this research fits into explanatory case study (Yin, 1993). The research issue is: *" How and why do research findings get into practical use?"* (Yin, 1993, p. 19)

3.4 Case Study Selection

The case study will focus on the research aim, which is to analyse how 4PL vendors meet clients' requirements and investigate the reasons for utilising 4PL. Basically, in 4PL relationships, there is a 4PL vendor, the physical service provider and on the other end, there is the client. The most important aspect of the case study will be that it will reveal issues on every side of the relationship with the interviews from each cluster. The physical service provider is important as well as the client and the 4PL vendor because at the end of the day, the physical service provider is the one that provides the actual physical service. The case study will shed light on events about how 4PL vendors meet clients' requirements and investigate the reasons for utilising 4PL. Research objectives, questions and research aim and the course of events will be traced in the case study.

Suitable 4PL vendors throughout the UK were approached with a case study request letter to conduct a case study. The case study request letter is available in the appendices. However, only one company approved participating in the case study. Unfortunately, this is a significant limitation for research dissertations because it is likely that most of the companies that are approached for case studies disapprove participation. See appendixes 1-4 for further detail.

Fourth Party Logistics

The reasons are usually confidentiality and time issues. Companies are either worried about confidentiality of data or simply do not have the time to participate. Therefore, the case study will be conducted with the VP Group Ltd. The VP Group Ltd. is an Essex based 4PL provider in the UK, operating in the UK, Poland, Latvia, Greece, Russia, China, Italy, Denmark and Lithuania. They were obviously approached due to being a 4PL vendor offering a number of services for the entire supply chain management. In this particular contract, the client is London based Chipmunka Group-Publishing-Foundation, which is a mental health publisher. The physical service provider is Lightning Source Inc.- a subsidiary of Ingram Industries Inc.-in the printing and publishing industry, which has production facilities both in the US and the UK. Chipmunka Group-Publishing-Foundation gets the service from the VP Group Ltd., which utilises Lightning Source Inc. to print and dispatch material for Chipmunka Group-Publishing-Foundation. The most important point of this case study is that it will be structured to evaluate the viewpoints of all parties in a particular contract. Therefore, interviews will be conducted with the 4PL provider, the client as well as the physical service provider to ensure that the practice will be dealt with from every angle. The information will be garnered not only from the 4PL provider's point of view but also its customer and the physical service provider through its dealings with them.

3.5 Data Collection Methods

Four interviews were conducted to develop the case study. Director of the 4PL vendor VP Group Ltd., the CEO of the client Chipmunka Group-Publishing-Foundation, the key account manager and the client services manager of the physical service provider were interviewed. The interviewees were chosen according to their possible contribution to the analysis of the theoretical framework. Director of the 4PL vendor contributed to the relationship management and strategic development and 4PL models, supplier-client selection. The CEO of the client contributed to all elements in the framework. Director and the CEO were chosen to be interviewed due to their high positions in the companies. Key account manager and client services manager of the physical service provider contributed to the relationship management and strategic development in the framework. Interviewees from the physical service provider were interviewed because their positions matched with the information they could provide to achieve the research aim, objectives, and questions.

3.5.1 Interviews

Interviews took place in Milton Keynes, UK on April 3, 2007. Milton Keynes was chosen due to the physical service provider Lightning Source Inc., being based in Milton Keynes. The interview with Lightning Source

Fourth Party Logistics

Inc. took place in their production facility, as part of a meeting together with the VP Group Ltd. This was interesting and beneficial because the negotiations and dealings between the two parties were observed in practice.

Key account manager Chris Kinsey and client services manager Andrea Mansell from Lightning Source Inc. were present in the meeting and contributed to the interviews by answering different questions. Key account manager was interviewed due to being an employee with a high position and being active in the decision making process with key clients. Client services manager contributed to questions about relationships with the clients and had significant input about relationship management and strategic development in the theoretical framework. The questions that were asked were about their role in 4PL outsourcing, their relationships with their clients, changing industry trends and the particular challenges in the business.

The interviews with the VP Group Ltd. and Chipmunka Group-Publishing-Foundation took place in a public place in Milton Keynes. The director Andrew Latchford from the VP Group Ltd. and the CEO Jason Pegler from Chipmunka Group-Publishing-Foundation contributed to the interviews. Andrew Latchford was interviewed due to being the director of the VP Group Ltd. and answered questions about the services of the

The Future Of Supply Chain Outsourcing?

company, adding value to services, supplier- client satisfaction, implementation process, relationship management and the challenges in the particular contract. The CEO Jason Pegler of Chipmunka Group-Publishing-Foundation is a consultant, public speaker, trainer, writer and publisher, known as one of the most inspirational mental health empowerment speakers in the world. He has written an autobiography on mental health of his generation "A Can of Madness", published in 2002. He gave insights about the mental health publishing, motives for utilising 4PL, relationships with the supplier, supplier selection and drawbacks and risks of utilising 4PL.

See appendices 5 for pattern matching study and questions.

3.5.2 Interview Question Design

Interview questions were asked to achieve the research aim, objectives and the research questions. There were 4 elements in the theoretical framework and the questions needed to contribute to the theoretical framework to reach the research aim, objectives and the research questions. Interview questions were designed according to which party contributed to which element of the framework.

The first interview was conducted with the client and started off with questions about their motives for utilising 4PL and followed with the questions about drawbacks and risks of utilising 4PL, 4PL models, supplier-client selection and relationship management and strategic development respectively. However, the last question was also about drawbacks and risks of utilising 4PL. The client contributed to all elements in the framework. Therefore, questions about all the elements of the theoretical framework were asked.

The second interview was conducted with the 4PL vendor and started off and finished with questions about relationship management and strategic development. Two questions were asked about 4PL models, supplier-client selection in between. The 4PL vendor contributed to relationship management and strategic development and 4PL models, supplier-client selection in the framework. Therefore, questions about those elements of the theoretical framework were put to the interviewees.

The third and fourth interviews were conducted with the key account manager and client services manager of the physical service provider. These questions were only about relationship management and strategic development because the physical service provider only had a role in that element of the framework.

Although every interview had certain roles in the theoretical framework, it was thought that all the interviews had an overall contribution to it, showing different viewpoints about the same case and dealing with the case from every angle. The interview questions could be found in the appendices.

3.6 Data Analysis Methods

One of the ways to link data to propositions is utilising pattern matching, whereby several pieces of information from the same case may be related to some theoretical proposition. It is one of the most promising approaches to compare and contrast findings (Yin, 1994).

Case studies are designed to examine whether theories would specify the operational chain of events leading to the relevant outcomes. In this research, the pattern matching analysis will enable to see the outcomes of the interview questions, which were designed to achieve the research aim, objectives and questions. The research aim, objectives and questions obviously were related to the theoretical framework in the literature review. Therefore, the pattern matching process will enable comparing and contrasting the outcomes with the theoretical framework in the literature review (Yin, 1993).

3.7 Chapter Summary

Research paradigms and methodologies, the case study types design and selection along with the interviews and data collection methods were presented in this chapter. All of these will help collect the relevant data and develop the theoretical framework further. The case study will reveal important aspects of 4PL practice and will be analysed with a pattern matching table to see whether there are any similarities or differences between the views of each party. In the discussion chapter, the data will be compared and contrasted with what was discovered in the literature review.

Chapter 4: Research Findings

4.0 Chapter Introduction

In this chapter, the results of the interviews according to the answers from the interviewees will be presented. It will have subsections reflecting different outcomes about each element in the theoretical framework. Elements of the theoretical framework will be analysed from different viewpoints. Four interviews were made in total: One with the client, one with the 4PL vendor and two interviews with the physical service provider. The answers will be compared and contrasted to see whether there are any similarities or differences between ways and perceptions of how companies do business. The pattern matching table in the appendices should be seen for the interview questions, answers and the summary.

4.1 Motives for Utilising 4PL

There was only one respondent for these questions because "motives for utilising 4PL" element in the theoretical framework was merely relevant for the client.

4.1.1 The Client- Chipmunka Group-Publishing-Foundation

The first three questions for the client company were about its motives for utilising 4PL services and the effect of 4PL on the way it did business. The CEO Jason Pegler of Chipmunka Group-Publishing-

The Future Of Supply Chain Outsourcing?

Foundation stated that less administration duties, better profits and the integration of stock were the motives to utilise 4PL services and these changed the way they did business. He also stated that they were able to free up the time in order to grow the company and deal with their core competency, which was to produce books.

Therefore they had positive cash flow, more mature products and the products were integrated to more places with no stock at all. One of the most important services that the 4PL vendor provided through the physical service provider was UK and US distribution.

He stated that his company literally had a free business in the USA because the physical service provider offered global distribution, which they would not be able to get without 4PL. Had they not been utilising 4PL services, they would have had bad cash flow, more stock, no sales guarantee and a risk of losing money if the books did not sell. There was always a risk if one had a lot of stock and could not sell it, but with 4PL, Chipmunka Group-Publishing-Foundation had product diversity in terms of units and volume without the risk of low sales.

His company was able get POD (print on demand) services through the physical service provider, which enabled the company to have the books printed when the order was put through via different channels such as Amazon EU, Bertram Books, or the company's own website. Therefore there was no risk of excess stock.

He stated that single orders- POD was the biggest motivation for utilising 4PL services.

4.2 Drawbacks and Risks of Utilising 4PL

Similar to the questions about "motives for utilising 4PL" element, there was only one respondent for these questions because "drawbacks and risks of utilising 4PL" element in the theoretical framework was also merely relevant for the client.

4.2.1 The Client- Chipmunka Group-Publishing-Foundation

Questions 4, 5, 6, 7 and 13 were about the problems the company encountered in the implementation process and afterwards, Pegler's perception of why they encountered such problems, how they dealt with those problems, compatibility issues and drawbacks and risks of utilising 4PL services.

Pegler stated that the most significant problem they encountered was learning the ways to set up files. Setting up files was crucial in the publishing industry because there was no interaction after the order was put through for printing. Therefore, the files had to be set up in the most appropriate way to have perfect results. Otherwise, the books came out faulty. When they first started working with Lightning Source Inc., their way of setting up files was slightly different to Lightning Source Inc.'s. Therefore, compatibility issue arose

The Future Of Supply Chain Outsourcing?

between the files that Chipmunka Group-Publishing-Foundation set up for publishing and Lightning Source Inc.'s file formats.

File structure, name and type of file needed to follow the physical service provider's guidelines to match with their computer system to prevent faulty production. Further, it was stated that the physical service provider changed their guidelines over time. Therefore, they had to keep their compatibility up to date to meet the provider's guidelines for file setups. It was Chipmunka's responsibility to feed correct files to the provider because there was no manual interaction whatsoever on the provider's side after they received the file for publishing. If there was a mistake, it was Chipmunka's fault, not the provider's.

However, Pegler stated that those problems were inevitable due to different ways of working, when one's just started doing business with another. Those problems were dealt with by understanding the help section in the provider's website. They needed to follow the guidelines in the help section and be very careful when they set up files for putting through. They had more than one person to check the final files before sending them to the publisher. It was stated that Chipmunka had a 10% failure, which was not bad for industry standards.

Another problem Pegler mentioned was the missing EDI link for the orders. Although, they were using EDI links for order integration, there might have been issues in the links occasionally. The technology integration and compatibility was not entirely there, therefore problems occurred occasionally.

Pegler mentioned slow growth as a drawback because they had a long-term business model. POD was mentioned as a new concept in publishing, therefore the technology links were not all there yet. However, the concept would improve over time as more providers started to implement POD services. It was said that they needed to be patient while the new concept developed and keep themselves up to date to fulfil customer needs.

On the contrary, he said that there was no risk involved because a huge company Ingram Industries Inc. that would never go out of business owned Lightning Source Inc. Lightning Source Inc. had Ingram Industries Inc.'s power behind them that enabled single order processing. As long as they offered single order processing, which they always would, Chipmunka had no risk. The risk of having excess stock was eliminated by single order processing.

4.3 4PL Models, Supplier- Client Selection

Unlike the questions about "motives for utilising 4PL" and "drawbacks and risks of utilising 4PL" elements, 4PL Models, Supplier- Client Selection element involved questions from two interviews, which conducted with the client and the 4PL vendor.

Therefore these two interviews will be analysed together to compare and contrast findings.

4.3.1 The Client- Chipmunka Group-Publishing-Foundation and The 4PL Vendor-The VP Group Ltd.

Questions 8, 9, 10 were about Chipmunka's choice of utilising 4PL instead of 3PL and how 4PL added value to their service. Pegler stated that they chose to utilise 4PL services instead of 3PL because 4PL offered a no risk business with long-term exponential growth and global distribution.

It was thought that a 3PL provider would not be able to offer global distribution because the EDI link was missing and 3PL providers did not how to deliver either. More importantly, a 3PL provider would not print a single order, which he stated as the real value his company got through 4PL. If one utilised 3PL, they started saving money when they spent more. However, there was a contradiction, because an individual book going through 4PL cost a lot more than to print, say 5000 through someone else, printed in traditional methods of lithographic transfer. The print runs of 5,000 are normal however the unit cost is 25% of POD, lead time is traditionally 3 weeks, while 24 hours is the norm with POD via Lightning Source Inc.

But it was hard to sell 5000 books and what did one do with 5000 books if they did not sell. It was going to cost a lot more than what they were worth to get people buy them. Unless a company had millions of capital to invest when it started doing business, it was best to go with 4PL in the first place. Therefore, except for utilising 4PL, publishers started making profit when they spent more.

These advantages of VP Group Ltd. and Lightning Source Inc. were significantly important in supplier selection. It was also stated that, they would have paid a fortune to get a place for the books in a store if they wanted to put a book in a bookshop. POD enabled a long-term business model for Chipmunka but with slow growth. An interesting point he mentioned was that Lightning Source Inc. did not realize how good they were. His perception was that they were not fully aware of how effective their business model was with single order processing, which ultimately was the real value for Chipmunka.

Questions 5 and 6 for the 4PL vendor were about how they chose their suppliers and how they brought relevant parties together to provide the entire service. Latchford stated that they needed to know their clients' needs first to see how many of the clients' needs were addressed by potential suppliers. Clients' needs came first. They understood the client's needs before they chose the appropriate suppliers for a particular client. Once they have done that, they looked for the most appropriate suppliers. It was important to understand what the suppliers could deliver. They saw whether the client's needs matched with what the suppliers could deliver. After this evaluation, the appropriate suppliers and the client were brought together and introduced to each other. That was how they brought relevant parties together to provide the entire service.

However, he stated that most of the time, there was not a match between what the client wanted and what the suppliers could deliver. That was why most partnerships did not work and most businesses closed down after a short period. Although, finding the perfect match was a significant challenge for VP Group Ltd., the client did not mention it, probably because of the fact that they didn't have to find the physical service provider.

That was the 4PL vendor's job to find the physical service provider and make them work together. The client's answers were particularly about this particular contract because they were only working with one 4PL vendor and one physical service provider. However, the 4PL vendor gave generic insights about 4PL because they were working with a number of suppliers to meet every single client's needs. That was the whole point of 4PL anyway. According to Latchford, being able to find the perfect match for their clients was one of the differences between VP Group Ltd. and other 4PL consultancies, because the others went with only suppliers' needs. Others only took what the supplier could deliver into account.

4.4 Relationship Management and Strategic Development

This element of the framework involved questions for all the parties in the relationship. Therefore, all three interviews will be analysed together in this section.

4.4.1 The Client- Chipmunka Group-Publishing-Foundation, the 4PL Vendor- The VP Group Ltd. and the Physical Service Provider- Lightning Source Inc.

Questions 11, 12 for the client were about relationship management and strategic development and the most important aspects of their relationships with the 4PL vendor. Pegler mentioned delivering with an EDI integration, single order processing and price as important issues in order of importance. Even though the EDI link was not fully there, he stated that the 4PL vendor through Lightning Source Inc. was able to deliver in the most convenient way with their single order processing facility.

Lightning Source Inc. offered them the best available contract as well as a good price. Therefore, Chipmunka chose to work with VP Group Ltd. and Lightning Source Inc. Understanding and communication were stated as the most important aspects of their relationship with the 4PL vendor. They had frequent communication with the supplier to maintain strong relationships. He said that the 4PL vendor understood

The Future Of Supply Chain Outsourcing?

Chipmunka's business model, what they were trying to achieve, understood what they did and why they did it.

All the questions for the 4PL vendor VP Group Ltd. except for questions 5 and 6, were about the services they offered their clients, value adding, core competencies, client satisfaction, challenges in 4PL business, which were all related to relationship management and strategic development. Director Andrew Latchford of the VP Group Ltd. stated that they offered consultancy to their clients and the most important value they added was understanding and integration. The client also had mentioned understanding and integration as important issues.

Latchford said that it was crucial that one understands the clients' business and what they were trying to achieve. The client also confirmed this statement. Top level service in real consultancy was "detail". VP Group Ltd., as opposed to traditional business models, found out what the problems were and delivered solutions. It was stated that others found the problems, but could not deliver solutions. He said that making it happen and delivering; not just finding the problems, were their most important differentiations over other consultancies.

They understood the clients' business even before they had meetings with them. They tried to have as few meetings as possible and focused on delivering rather than just talking about issues. Understanding, delivering and integration were their core competencies.

Communication also was the key to how they maintained strong relationships with suppliers, like the client also mentioned. By talking to the physical service provider and customer and making suggestions about solutions, they maintained satisfaction for their services. He stated that one should have no preconceptions, find out what is going on in the world, read relevant literature, speak to people in order to deliver solutions and meet changing industry trends.

He also mentioned listening to what user groups say as of great importance. Further, he thought that they drove industry trends with different kinds of books from Chipmunka by their media coverage. It was said that 4PL business was proactive and had a dynamic business model as opposed to 3PL, which was reactive.

Latchford mentioned file compatibility issues as problems in the implementation process like Pegler did. They dealt with those problems by following the guidelines on a regular basis and with the help from both sides (Chipmunka and Lightning Source Inc.). Apart from file compatibility issues, they had no problems. He said that the rest of it was simple, provided that they understood what the physical service provider could deliver and what the client was trying to achieve. However, marketing and PR were found as the two of the most challenging parts of 4PL business. He said that the least challenging was delivering, which was completely the reverse for the big consultancy firms.

VP Group Ltd. tried to deliver what they could as opposed to others, who tried to deliver everything. They only took on contracts that they could deliver solutions. But others would take on anything just for the sake of it, for PR and marketing; however couldn't deliver solutions. That was why VP Group Ltd. lacked in marketing and PR and others did not. However, the client did not mention marketing and PR probably because these weren't their job. Like it was mentioned earlier on, the 4PL vendor gave generic insights as opposed to the client, who mentioned characteristics of this particular case. It was not that the others did not try to deliver.

They tried, but they couldn't deliver. Big consultancy firms charged for the solutions they knew nothing about, Latchford stated. They charged for just advising how to deliver. However, they didn't deliver it for you. Further, it was not their responsibility to deliver solutions. He said that it was a waste of time if one got involved with big names in the 4PL business because contracts were taken on just for the sake of marketing and PR.

Therefore, 80% of invitations were rejected due to being selective and not taking on every contract. Most of the potential clients were not flexible and set strict requirements. If the clients were resistant to change , VP Group Ltd. was unable to match solutions. As a result, they rejected the invitation.

The rejection issue was also mentioned in 4PL Models, Supplier- Client Selection element. Flexibility issue created another challenge for the VP Group Ltd. because they would not take on a client just for the sake of marketing and PR. Their main aim was to deliver solutions. This was mentioned about how they saw strategic development and relationship management. When they took on a client, they tried to give them the best deal available, tried to deliver solutions without wasting time. They achieved this with communication, an open mind and flexibility.

Key account manager Chris Kinsey answered questions 1, 3, 5 for the physical service provider, Lightning Source Inc. They were about their role in 4PL outsourcing, how they maintained 4PL vendor satisfaction and the most important service that they could provide through 4PL. Kinsey stated that Lightning Source Inc. provided POD services, order fulfillment and dispatching for the publishing industry. Above all, POD services- single copy order fulfillment via multiple channels such as Amazon EU, Bertram Books, Gardner Books Ltd., etc. with a global distribution, was the most important service. Lightning Source Inc. worked with the principle; order before the printing. Therefore, they provided the advantage of no stock. This service had also been mentioned by the client as the real value his company got through 4PL. They printed books as the orders came through. It was stated that they maintained satisfaction with this unique service, multiple channels, reasonable systems and quality. They had regular meetings with clients and production editors, listened to what user groups were looking for and had EDI links for order processing. Their dispatch facility had a real time barcoding system, which was linked with clients' accounts. This information could be reached from their website at any time. Therefore, clients could see their order status in real time. This user-friendly process reduced the amount of admin work, which had also been one of the motives for the client to utilise 4PL.

Questions 2, 4, 6 and 7 were answered by the client services manager Andrea Mansell from Lightning Source Inc. These questions revealed challenges for maintaining satisfaction for their services, how they met changing industry trends, which were issues about relationship management and strategic development. Mansell mentioned delivering, making sure the deals reacted with the 4PL vendor and meeting the expectations as the challenges for maintaining satisfaction. They dealt with these challenges with communication, EDI links and understanding what their clients were after for their own clients. These had also been mentioned by the client and the 4PL vendor.

Lightning Source Inc. kept up to date with the industry by attending meetings, industry conferences, forums as well as conducting surveys (questionnaires). They needed to know what was going on in the industry and evaluate issues before their competitors did. Being up to date enabled them to react to clients needs and offer what their competitors could not with a flexible fashion. Flexibility, client feedback evaluation and customised offers were important points in relationship management and strategic development. Therefore, they were flexible, open minded and gave great value to client feedback. Single order processing was integrated with EDI links through multiple channels, which resulted in strong relationships with clients.

4.5 Chapter Summary

The pattern matching analysis enabled the author to reveal important issues in the theoretical framework, which in this research were "relationship management and strategic development", "4PL models, supplier-client selection", "motives for utilising 4PL" and "drawbacks and risks of utilising 4PL".

Understanding, technology integrated links and delivering were mentioned by all parties about their relationships between each other and about how they maintained strong relationships. The 4PL vendor's most important service was delivering, which was particularly delivered through the physical service provider to the client. It was interesting that Latchford of the VP Group said that delivering was the least challenging part of the business whereas Andrea Mansell of Lightning Source Inc. stated that as the most challenging part. The 4PL vendor brought relevant parties together to provide the entire service by understanding what their suppliers produced and what the clients wanted.

Both the physical service provider and the client mentioned POD service with a global distribution through multiple channels as the most important service they got or provided according to their position. Both the 4PL vendor and the client mentioned file compatibility issues in relation with problems, drawbacks and risks of the 4PL service. A help from both sides along with following the guidelines in the physical service provider's website were mentioned as a solution.

Flexibility was important for the 4PL vendor and the physical service provider about how they did business. Pegler of Chipmunka mentioned less administration duties, better profits, integration of stock, product diversity in terms of units and volume and a no risk business about the motivation for utilising 4PL services and about how they chose their supplier. He also said that they had a no risk business because the company who owned Lightning Source Inc. was so large. Another important aspect of the relationships mentioned by all parties was communication.

There is an unexpected amount of interaction between vendor and supplier, often in 4PL. Both parties look to increase margins or expectation levels for their business. They treat 4PL as a whole and work together to achieve better outcomes rather than just focus on their part.

Chapter 5: Discussion

5.0 Chapter Introduction

In this chapter, a discussion between the elements of theoretical framework in the literature review and the findings of the case study will be presented. It will have sections discussing the each element of the framework, the relevant findings from the relevant parties. Elements of the theoretical framework in the literature review and the findings will be compared and contrasted in order to see whether there are differences and similarities between what was discovered with the case study and what was in the literature review. It will then conclude with a chapter summary, which will summarise the whole discussion.

5.1 Motives for Utilising 4PL

There was only one respondent for these questions because "motives for utilising 4PL" element in the theoretical framework was merely relevant for the client. Therefore, this element will be discussed from the client's point of view only.

5.1.1 The Client- Chipmunka Group-Publishing-Foundation

Motives for utilising 4PL mentioned in the literature review were cost reduction, adding value, removal of key problems of 3PL, efficient information flow, change management and collaboration, leanness and agility and e- supply chain.

Fourth Party Logistics

In the case study the client did not directly mention cost reduction. However, better profits and a positive cash flow were mentioned as financial motivations. The client also stated that they had in effect free business in the USA with the opportunity of global distribution.

This might also be considered as a financial motivation resulting in cost reductions. Supply chain integration was cited as the 4PL vendor's primary responsibility in the literature in Bade and Mueller (1999). In the case study, it was discovered that integration of stock was crucial for the client. Supply chain integration was an important point, however, through integration of stock. The client was able to do business without any stock at all, further with product diversity through 4PL. However, confidential issues about the details of gain-share agreements were not mentioned by the client, which were cited in Trecha (2002) in the literature to increase the costs of utilising 4PL.

Improved customer service by allowing companies to focus on their core competency was mentioned under the "cost reduction" title cited in Vaidyanathan (2005). The client was also able to improve customer service and free up the time in order to grow the company and focus on its core competency. Information integrated technology links, coordination and communication mentioned under "value adding" cited in Love (2004) and Van Hoek and Chong (2001) in the literature, generated important aspects of their relationships with the 4PL vendor.

The biggest motivation for the client to utilise 4PL was the POD service, which the 3PL couldn't provide. Meeting expectations, providing the optimal combination of technology, transportation and the need for more intelligent solutions generated the problems of 3PL under the title "removal of the key problems of 3PL" in the literature. Therefore it could be understood that the removal of the key problems of 3PL was one of the main reasons for the client to go for 4PL, which eventually provided the POD service. Figure 2.2: The 4PL value proposition (Foster, 1999a, p.62), in the literature explains all the above about enhanced product quality, availability, fixed capital reduction, customer service performance, reduced inventory, etc., which ultimately lead to reduced capital investment, increased profitability and greater shareholder value.

All the motives mentioned above also were results of "efficient information flow", which was a title under "motives for utilising 4PL" in the literature. Information flow was one of the most important points to achieve what were mentioned above about the process. EDI links and the Internet cited in Gattorna and Walters (1996) and Lankford (2004), made it easier to manage inventory levels, reduce administration duties, provided advantages of speed, decrease paper and labour usage, reduced costs and provided better tracking. They enabled synchronisation and easy access to information via user-friendly applications. 4PL was approached as a centralised "optimisation tool" by Kerr (2006) in the literature for coordination and collaboration. In fact, the 4PL vendors centrally managed everything related to the supply chain. Inventory and production management should be handled with leanness and agility where appropriate and this was achieved through efficient information flow. Orders are fed through to the physical service provider via the EDI link and the physical service provider manages the production and inventory levels according to this information. Therefore, nothing should go wrong in the network with efficient information links. However, the client and the 4PL vendor mentioned compatibility as a problem in the EDI link in the drawbacks and relationship management and strategic development elements. Information network would only work provided the systems were compatible. All of these were crucial aspects of competitive advantage. Although issues about information flow were mentioned in the relationship management and strategic development element in the case study, they were also important for motives for utilising 4PL. After all, all the elements of the framework were overall aspects related to the bigger picture. Therefore, there would obviously be an overlap between them.

5.2 Drawbacks and Risks of Utilising 4PL

There was only one respondent for these questions because "drawbacks and risks of utilising 4PL" element in the theoretical framework was merely relevant for the client. Therefore, this element will be discussed from the client's point of view only.

5.2.1 The Client- Chipmunka Group-Publishing-Foundation

Improved customer service and profitability cited in Foster (1999b) in the literature review were thought about the main reasons to go for 4PL. It was also discovered in the case study that improved customer service and profitability were two of the main reasons to utilise 4PL. High switching costs and long-term partnerships cited in Gattorna (1998) in the literature were mentioned as drawbacks of utilising 4PL. It was hard to change partners due to high switching costs. Conversely, it was discovered that the client had no switching costs at all, further along with a free business in the USA via global distribution through multiple channels.

The client never mentioned changing partners anyway, or decoupling the production because they were happy with the results of the particular relationship. It must be noted that decoupling would not happen at the volumes of books currently sold(under 300 per book , per month). A coupling reversal happens where the book

Fourth Party Logistics

on offer is no longer main stream, and moves to POD, as a long tail process (total sales are as much as the total print run in the first 2 years, however over a longer period- hence the term)

Therefore, utilising 4PL actually saved them money rather than cost much more. A long-term partnership was mentioned as a drawback, in the case study, though in terms of slow growth; not due to switching costs.

Loss of control over the processes cited in Richardson (2005) was discovered as a drawback of utilising 4PL in the literature. For instance, head of global accounts for the logistics division for UPS Logistics, Andreas Janetzko, stated that the logistics directors he talked to often reacted defensively to any mention of 4PL (Tierney, 2004). *"They feel under threat at the thought of an outside organisation managing their overall logistics activities, applying intelligence and orchestrating everything that goes on. They feel that's their job"* (Tierney, 2004, p.18).

However, this issue was not mentioned at all by the client as a drawback. Moreover, it was stated that passing the administration duties and control on to the 4PL vendor was a great advantage of utilising 4PL, because it saved time to focus on their core competency. Therefore, passing the administration control on to the 4PL vendor was a motive for the client.

One of the other drawbacks discovered in the case study was the compatibility issue. The client stated that the most significant problem they encountered was learning the ways to set up files. Setting up files was crucial in the publishing industry because there was no interaction after the order was put through for printing. Therefore, it was the client's responsibility to feed correct files to the physical service provider. Moreover, the physical service provider changed their guidelines for file setups over time according to changing industry dynamics. As cited in Gattorna (1998) in the literature review; changing industry dynamics may make obsolete some or all of the services that the 4PL organisation originally provides.

Another rare problem the client mentioned was the missing EDI link. It was also thought that the client had no risks because the physical service provider was owned by a huge company and had their power behind them.

5.3 4PL Models, Supplier- Client Selection

Unlike the questions about "motives for utilising 4PL" and "drawbacks and risks of utilising 4PL" elements, "4PL Models, Supplier- Client Selection" element involved questions from two interviews, which were conducted with the client and the 4PL vendor. Therefore, the views of these two will be discussed together.

5.3.1 The Client- Chipmunka Group-Publishing-Foundation and The 4PL Vendor-The VP Group Ltd.

4PL Models, Supplier- Client Selection element in the literature review focused on issues regarding how to outsource, how should suppliers and clients choose their partners rather than why. It was mentioned that different products and markets would have different requirements (Kerr, 2006). Unfortunately, from the client's point of view, this case study in this research only reflected the printing and publishing industry, because the particular contract was of that particular industry. Therefore, this research had the limitation of reflecting results of a case of printing and publishing industry.

However, the results could be broadened with the 4PL vendor's contribution, because they work not only with the companies in the printing and publishing industry but also with others. Therefore, the 4PL vendor had a broader view of 4PL.

It was stated in the literature that logistics outsourcing had been utilised for many years, but expect 4PL, it couldn't go further than transportation and warehousing (Hertz and Alfredsson, 2003). This statement reflected what the client has said about their choice of utilising 4PL instead of 3PL, because they were looking for services beyond transportation and warehousing. They said that the EDI link was missing in 3PL and 3PL couldn't provide single order processing, which were the real value they got through 4PL.

A methodology called analytic network process (ANP) based final selection by Jharkharia and Shankar (2007), was presented in the literature as a selection model, which identified four major criteria named compatibility, cost, quality and reputation, that are further supported by four sub-criteria. Although these criteria, except for reputation, were mentioned by the client, they were not mentioned as part of a final selection model. Actually neither the client nor the 4PL vendor mentioned any selection models. These criteria were not mentioned in the 4PL Models, supplier- client selection element either, but in motives for utilising 4PL, drawbacks and risks of utilising 4PL and relationship management and strategic development. Therefore, these criteria were also important for supplier selection, only in another way.

There were other issues mentioned by the client such as the unawareness of the physical service provider of how effective their business model was and that it actually cost much more in ways other than utilising 4PL, which did not take place in the literature.

One of the most relevant aspects about how the 4PL vendor chose its suppliers was that the client's need came first. The 4PL vendor needed to know their client's needs first to see how many of those needs were addressed by potential suppliers. This point also was cited in Foggin *et al.,* (2004) in the literature. Foggin *et al.,* (2004) was also cited for that most of the relationships failed due to lack of communication and misunderstandings, which was also mentioned by the 4PL vendor. He said that most partnerships failed because there was not a match between what the client wanted and what the supplier could deliver. Moreover, he found this as a significant challenge for his company.

However, the 4PL vendor didn't state that they were using quantitative tools, benchmarking techniques or performance measures. They made their evaluation after initial investigation. Communication and understanding were key points about supplier selection in the case study.

5.4 Relationship Management and Strategic Development

This element of the theoretical framework was only researched from the 4PL vendor's side in the literature review due to the limitation of secondary data. There was no secondary data particularly related to the physical service providers or clients involved in 4PL, except for the surveys cited in Biederman (2005, p.29) and Accenture (2004).

However interviews were conducted with the physical service provider and the client as well. Due to the overlap between the elements of the framework and the interview opportunities, findings in this case also reflected viewpoints of the client and the physical service provider about relationship management and strategic development. Although there was this limitation in the literature, this research is unique in terms of having added the client and the physical service provider in the case study. Two questions were asked to the client about this particular element of the framework. Therefore, the client's and the physical service provider's views will be discussed as well as the 4PL vendor's. However, there will not be separate sections for each of them.

The relationship between all parties was collaborative, but not mutually exclusive to each other.

5.4.1 The Client- Chipmunka Group-Publishing-Foundation, the 4PL Vendor- The VP Group Ltd. and the Physical Service Provider- Lightning Source Inc.

The balance of adaptation and standardisation was cited in Hertz and Alfredsson (2003) in the literature. Integration, understanding and detail were important for the 4PL vendor. Communication and having no preconceptions were also mentioned as the key to how the 4PL vendor maintained strong relationships with suppliers and clients.

The 4PL vendor didn't directly mention standardisation and adaptation, but he gave clues about adaptation. It could be understood that their service relied on adaptation from the statements above. They needed to understand what the suppliers could deliver and what the client was trying to achieve. Therefore, they needed to adapt their services to what the client wanted with customised solutions for each of them. A customised solution for each client was also mentioned by the physical service provider.

Figure 2.6: TPL firms classified according to abilities of general problem solving and customer adaptation (Hertz and Alfredsson, 2003, p.141) classified providers according to abilities of general problem solving and customer adaptation. 4PL relationships fitted into the customer developer type of relationships, which involved a high integration with the customer.

The Future Of Supply Chain Outsourcing?

These types of relationships were the most advanced and difficult, often in the form of taking over the whole supply chain operations for the client. Problem solving ability and customer adaptation were at high levels. This exactly reflected what was discovered in the case study. The client stated delivering with an EDI integration, single order processing and price as important issues. He also mentioned understanding and communication.

Therefore, he confirmed "adaptation" as the key point in relationship management and strategic development. File compatibility issues were mentioned as problems in the implementation process. As they tried to overcome those problems with the help from both sides, they developed their skills and core competencies to increase customer adaptation. This mutual learning developed their problem solving ability, increased integration and resulted in a higher level of commitment, which were cited in Hertz and Alfredsson (2003) in the literature about relationship management and strategic development.

It was interesting to find out what the 4PL vendor had to say about flexibility, PR, marketing and about the big brands in the consultancy industry. These issues took place in research findings chapter. However, they weren't discovered in the literature. As a result of the interviews with the physical service provider, their perceptions about relationship management and strategic development were also discovered. They also mentioned communication, understanding, single order processing, customised offers, flexibility as their core competencies. In the end, it was understood that similar characteristics of the relationship were important for all the parties. This was inevitable anyway, because all the parties came together to meet each other's requirements on a particular contract. The client chose to work with the other parties because they found what they were looking for.

5.5 Limitations of the Research

Limitations of this research were availability of secondary data about 4PL in the literature and the difficulty in finding the organisations for the case study. However, the case study of printing and publishing industry was conducted eventually with the help of the 4PL vendor and participations of the other parties. Therefore, this research only reflects findings for the printing and publishing case.

However it must be noted that while other 4PL providers or solution providers did not respond, this research is very much leading edge.

5.6 Chapter Summary

Differences and similarities between what was discovered with the case study and what was in the literature review were analysed in the discussion chapter. Eventually, it was found out that there were some similarities between the elements of the framework and case study findings as well as some different issues.

Some points mentioned in the findings were mentioned under different titles in the literature review whereas some others had an exact match to where they were mentioned in the literature. Moreover, some case study findings did not take place in the literature and there were some oppositions or different perceptions to what was stated in the literature. For instance, efficient information flow was mentioned under the motives for utilising 4PL but it was discovered that this particular aspect was not only a motive for the client but also crucial for the supplier and the physical service provider about relationship management and strategic development. Moreover, this particular aspect was mentioned as a drawback of utilising 4PL in the case study.

These differentiations were inevitable because of the overlap between the elements of the framework and the nature of this research. Qualitative research would not provide straight answers nor would the answers be physically measurable. Therefore, different perceptions about the same subject are inevitable. It all differs according to interpretation and/or the particular relationship, contract that is being researched. The most obvious overlap was in the relationship management and strategic development element due to the interview question design. However, this overlap should not be considered as bad. Different viewpoints were discovered as a result.

It must be noted again that ALL parties where working together, not apart the adoption of the 4PL standards and working methods. Where just like BPO and reengineering, however they have a deeper more profound affect on not only relationships but also the businesses and they way they interacted together.

Chapter 6: Conclusions and Recommendations

6.1 Conclusions

In this chapter, the author will go back to the research aim, objectives, and research questions to see how the research aim and objectives were achieved and whether the research questions were answered. These provided the base for the research and they will be evaluated with what was achieved at the end of this research dissertation. A full list of the research aim, objectives, and research questions is available in the introduction chapter.

Two research questions along with a number of objectives were identified to achieve the research aim, which was "to analyse the reasons for utilising 4PL and investigate how 4PL vendors meet clients' requirements". Two of the most significant research objectives were "To conduct a literature review to reveal the key issues in 4PL and to identify and conduct a suitable case study to reflect 4PL practice".

The contents of the literature review and the case study were determined accordingly, to achieve the research aim. Therefore, the literature review was structured according to the research aim, objectives and research questions. It was then supported with a case study to discuss and evaluate what the literature review reflected and what actually happened in practice.

Fourth Party Logistics

The research questions were: "How do 4PL vendors meet the growing complexity of expectations and demands?" and "Why do clients utilise 4PL?" These were answered via the literature review in relevant chapters and sections with a number of academic references, books and figures. The type of the research questions suited for a case study as the research methodology.

Therefore, they were then supported with a case study to compare and contrast the literature review with the actual 4PL practice. Interview questions in the case study were also designed according to the research questions, objectives and the research aim. The entire research dissertation could be taken as the answers to the research questions. Although the answers to the research questions were quite broad, they might as well be answered in a simple way. The 4PL vendor met the growing complexity of expectations and demands by communication, integration, efficient information flow, customisation and delivering; in short by their core competencies. Analysing the core competencies of 4PL vendors was one of the research objectives. Therefore, these also reflect an objective and could be given as a simple answer to how 4PL vendors met the growing complexity of expectations and demands.

The second research question: "Why do clients utilise 4PL?" was also answered in the "motives for utilising 4PL" section of the literature review. The titles of that particular section could be taken as a simple answer to this question. These were cost reduction, adding value, removal of key problems of 3PL, efficient information flow, leanness and agility, etc. The answer to how 4PL vendors met the growing complexity of expectations and demands was also the reason for the clients to utilise 4PL. They utilised 4PL, because they found what they were looking for and what they were looking for was the core competencies of the 4PL vendor. What the client particularly mentioned as their motives for utilising 4PL were less administration duties, better profits, integration of stock, product diversity and POD service with global distribution. The research questions were also answered in other elements of the framework due to the overlap in between the elements.

One of the objectives: "To analyse important aspects of 4PL type of relationships", was achieved through 4PL models, supplier- client selection and relationship management and strategic development elements. Moreover, relationship management and strategic development element revealed views not only from the client and the 4PL vendor, but also from the physical service provider. Thus, physical service provider's contribution to the relationship was also analysed. Having made interviews with all the parties enabled the author to analyse the 4PL concept from every angle. In the end, the research aim was achieved by answering the research questions and reaching the objectives.

6.2 Recommendations
6.2.1 Operational Recommendations

There are certain things that a company should consider if they want to utilise 4PL for their supply chain management. Important issues about the motives of utilising that were discovered in this research should be taken into account. Although the reasons for considering 4PL utilisation might be different for every single company, there are certain important points to look for in a 4PL vendor.

Understanding, communication and integration were mentioned by all parties in this research as very important points for adding value, meeting requirements and motivations for utilising 4PL. Fast growing technology gives a lot of opportunities to companies in terms of communication and information flow. It gives advantages of speed and less administration duties and makes life easier for business people. However, it can be a burden if compatibility is not there. Technology is rapidly changing; therefore providers should be up to date to keep their systems compatible with other recognised systems. Clients also should look for suppliers that utilise compatible systems not only with them but also with their own suppliers. It is a prerequisite to avoid unforeseen problems in advance.

4PL vendors should understand their clients business and what they are trying achieve. They should be able to deliver solutions for them and carry their business ahead. They should also treat their clients' business as their own because partnerships are all about gaining and sharing. Vendors should be able to provide the best breed of their own suppliers and match what their clients want with what their suppliers can provide. Otherwise, it will be waste of time for all parties. Vendors and clients might use evaluation and benchmarking techniques or selection models to choose the best one available to work with. However, they should also be flexible to be able make trade offs where necessary and trust whom they work with. There will always be some risks in business life. Thus, they should see whether the outcomes outweigh the risks.

6.2.2 Recommendations for Further Research

A number of further research areas can be identified for the topic 4PL that was presented in this research. These might be as follows:

- 4PL models, supplier-client selection might be investigated further to see whether there are any other models utilised in practice.
- Case studies for different industries can be conducted to see whether what was discovered for the printing and publishing case in this research is relevant in other cases in other industries.

Fourth Party Logistics

- The element of "final customer" might be added to the case study in this research to discover their views of the 4PL service.

References

Accenture, (2004), Driving high performance outsourcing: Best practices from the masters- Executive survey results, *Accenture,* 2004

Aitken, J., Christopher, M. and Towill D., (2002), Understanding, Implementing and Exploiting Agility and Leanness, *International Journal of Logistics,* Vol: 5, Issue 1, pp.59-74

Andersson, D. and Norrman, A., (2002), Procurement of Logistics Services—A Minutes Work or a Multi-Year Project?, *European Journal of Purchasing and Supply Management,* Vol:8 Issue 3, p.3

Article, (2000), Companies Fail to Adopt E-Supply-Chains, *Logistics & Transport Focus,* Vol: 2 Issue 4, pp.10-10

Bade, D.J. and Mueller, J.K., (1999), New for the Millennium: 4PL, *Transportation and Distribution,* Vol: 40 Issue 2, p.78

Biederman, D., (2005), Growth Business, *Journal of Commerce,* Vol: 6 Issue 23, p.29

BIG, (2004), 4PL- What Is It?, *Business Intelligence Group Pty. Ltd.,* pp.1-21

Fourth Party Logistics

Cabodi C., (2004), 4PL: The Right Choice for All Logistics Service Providers and Shippers?, *Frost&Sullivan Market Insight*, pp.1-2

Christopher, M., (2000), The Agile Supply Chain: Competing in Volatile Markets, *Industrial Marketing Management*, Vol: 29 Issue 1, pp.37-44

Christopher, M. and Towill D., (2001), An Integrated Model for the Design of Agile Supply Chains, *International Journal of Physical Distribution & Logistics Management*, Vol: 31 Issue 4, pp.235-246

Collis, J. and Hussey, R., (2003), *Business Research- A Practical Guide for Undergraduate and Postgraduate Students*, Palgrave Macmillan

Cooper, M. C., Lambert, D. M. and Pagh, J. D., (1997), Supply Chain Management: More Than a New Name for Logistics, *The International Journal of Logistics Management,* Vol:8 Issue 1, pp.1-14

Foggin, J. H., Mentzer, J. T. and Monroe, C. L., (2004), A Supply Chain Diagnostic Tool, *International Journal of Physical Distribution & Logistics Management*, Vol: 34 Issue 10, pp.827-855

Foster, T. A., (1999a), Who's In Charge Around Here?, *Logistics Management & Distribution Report*, Vol: 38 Issue 6, p.61

The Future Of Supply Chain Outsourcing?

Foster, T. A., (1999b), 4PLs: The next generation for supply chain outsourcing?, *Logistics Management & Distribution Report*, Vol: 38 Issue 4, p.35

Gattorna, J. L., (1998), *Strategic Supply Chain Alignment, Best Practice in Supply Chain Management,* Gower Publishing Limited, England

Gattorna, J.L. and Walters, D.W., (1996), *Managing the Supply Chain, a Strategic Perspective*, Macmillan Press Ltd.

Harris, A., (2004), Reaping the Rewards of Agile Thinking, *Manufacturing Engineer*, Vol: 83 Issue 6, pp.24-27

Hertz, S. and Alfredsson, M., (2003), Strategic Development of Third Party Logistics Providers, *Industrial Marketing Management*, Vol: 32 Issue 2, pp.139-149

Jharkharia, S. and Shankar, R., (2007), Selection of Logistics Service Provider: An Analytic Network Process (ANP) Approach, *The International Journal of Management Science*, Vol: 35 Issue 3, pp.274-289

Jones, H., (2001), Success on the Highways, *Frontline Solutions Europe*, Vol: 10 Issue 5, p.20

Jones, R.M and Towill, D.R., (1999), Using the

Fourth Party Logistics

Information Decoupling Point to Improve Supply Chain Performance, *The International Journal of Logistics Management*, Vol: 10 Issue 2, pp.13-26

Kampstra, R.P., Ashayeri, J. and Gattorna J.L., (2006), Realities of Supply Chain Collaboration, *The International Journal of Logistics Management*, Vol: 17 Issue 3, pp.312-330

Kerr, J., (2006), What's the Right Role for Global 3PLs?, *Logistics Management*, Vol: 45 Issue 2, pp.51-57

Lankford, W. M., (2004), Supply Chain Management and the Internet, *Online Information Review*, Vol: 28 Issue 4, pp.301-305

Lee, H. L., Padmanabhan, V. and Whang, S., (1997), Information Distortion in a Supply Chain: The Bullwhip Effect, *Management Science*, Vol: 43 Issue 4, pp.546-558

Love, J., (2004), 3PL/4PL- Where Next?, *Logistics & Transport Focus*, Vol: 6 Issue 3, pp.18-21

Menzefricke, K., (2004), Fourth Party Logistics Transforms Logistics from a Cost Proposition to a Value Proposition, *Frost&Sullivan Market Insight*, pp.1-2

Naylor, J.B., Naim, M.M. and Berry, D. (1999),

The Future Of Supply Chain Outsourcing?

Leagility: Interfacing the Lean and Agile Manufacturing Paradigm in the Total Supply Chain, *International Journal of Production Economics*, Vol: 62, pp. 107-18

Onge, S. A., (2002), Outsourcing Logistics?, *Frontline Solutions*; Dec2002, Vol. 3 Issue 13, p.15

Pant, S., Sethi, R. and Bhandari, M., (2003), Making Sense of the E-supply Chain Landscape: An Implementation Framework, *International Journal of Information Management*, Vol: 23 Issue 3, pp.201-221

Perry, C., (1998), Processes of a Case Study Methodology for Postgraduate Research in Marketing, *European Journal of Marketing*, Vol: 32 Issue 9/10, pp. 785-802

Razzaque, M. A. and Sheng C. C., (1998), Outsourcing of Logistics Functions: A Literature Survey, *International Journal of Physical Distribution & Logistics Management*, Vol: 28 Issue 2/3, p.89

Richardson, H. L., (2005), What are You Willing to Give Up?, *Logistics Today*, Vol: 46 Issue 3, pp.27-29

Roberts, S., (2003), Fourth Party Politics, *Frontline Solutions Europe*, Vol: 12 Issue 5, p.14

Schwartz, E., (2003), The Logistics Handoff, *InfoWorld*, Vol: 25 Issue 44, pp.53-58

Singh, J., (1996), The Importance of Information Flow within the Supply Chain, *Logistics Information Management*, Vol: 9 Issue 4, pp.28-30

Tierney, S., (2004a), New Frost&Sullivan Study Bids to Bring Logistics to the Four, *Supply Chain Europe*, Vol: 13 Issue 3, pp.44-45

Tierney, S., (2004b), Now There are Real 4PL Possibilities, *Supply Chain Europe*, Vol: 13 Issue 5, pp.16-18

Trecha, S. J., (2002), Incentivized Buyer and Supplier Alliances Drive Continuous Supply Chain Improvement, *Pulp & Paper*, Vol: 76 Issue 11, pp.51-54

Vaidyanathan, G., (2005), A Framework for Evaluating Third-Party Logistics, *Communications of the ACM*, Vol: 48 Issue 1, pp.89-94

Van Hoek, R. I., (2001), E-supply Chains-Virtually Non-Existing, *Supply Chain Management: An International Journal*, Vol: 6 Issue 1, pp.21-28

Van Hoek, R. I. and Chong I., (2001), Epilogue: UPS Logistics – Practical Approaches to the E-supply Chain,

The Future Of Supply Chain Outsourcing?

International Journal of Physical Distribution & Logistics Management, Vol: 31 Issue 6, p.643

Yin, R. K., (1993), *Applications of Case Study Research*, Sage Publications Inc.

Yin, R. K., (1994), *Case Study Research- Design and Methods- 2nd edition*, Sage Publications Inc.

Yin, R. K., (2003), *Applications of Case Study Research- 2nd edition*, Sage Publications Inc.

Appendices

Appendix 1: Case Study Request Letter

Dear Sir/Madam,

I am a postgraduate student studying Msc International Business in the University of Salford. Currently, I am writing my research dissertation about 4PL (fourth party logistics). I have just finished the final draft of my literature review. At this stage, I need to approach a company in the UK to conduct a case study, which consists of interviews with a few members of the company. My research is based on the motives for utilising 4PL, supplier/client selection, relationship management and strategic development, and drawbacks and risks of utilising 4PL. I am analysing the core competencies of 4PL vendors and whether utilising 4PL can be a competitive leverage point. Therefore, your experiences about your supplier/client selection, why your clients/suppliers work with you and relationships with your suppliers/clients will be very helpful. I am sure you or your colleagues have done similar research when you were a student. Thus, your help will be for a good cause and information you provide will be anonymous unless you want your name mentioned in the research. You might have concerns about the confidentiality of information. Information will be kept confidential and will not be forwarded to third parties. I have found your company from various internet database searches and I would like to conduct my case study with you if you are available. It will be

The Future Of Supply Chain Outsourcing?

much appreciated if you could spare a few hours of your day for my case study. Please let me know whether you might be available and if so, when you will be available for me to come and visit you for the interviews. Thanks for your attention. Do not hesitate to contact me for further enquiries. You will find my contact details below.

Yours sincerely
Serafettin Kutlu
University of Salford-Msc International Business
Address: 7 Lower Park Road Carfax Court Flat 3 Victoria Park Manchester M14 5RQ
S.Kutlu@pgt.salford.ac.uk

Appendix 2: Interview Questions

For the client- Chipmunka Group-Publishing-Foundation

1. How has utilising 4PL changed the way you do business?
2. How has your provision of 4PL changed since you started utilising the service?
3. How were you encouraged to utilise 4PL services, what were your motives?
4. What were the problems you encountered?
5. Why do you think you encountered those particular problems, and how did you deal with them?
6. Were there any compatibility issues?
7. If there were compatibility issues, did you introduce any new applications for your supply chain management?
8. Why did you choose to utilise 4PL instead of 3PL?
9. How do you think utilising 4PL adds value to your service?
10. How did you choose your 4PL supplier?
11. What are the most important aspects of your relationships with your 4PL suppliers?
12. How do you maintain strong relationships with your suppliers?
13. What are the drawbacks and risks in utilising 4PL services?

Appendix 3: Interview Questions

For the 4PL vendor- The VP Group Ltd.

1. Which services do you offer your clients for their overall supply chain management?
2. What is the most important differentiation (value) that you offer to your clients?
3. How do you add value to service levels?
4. What do you think your core competencies are?
5. How do you choose your suppliers?
6. How do you bring relevant parties together to provide the entire service?
7. How do you meet changing industry trends?
8. How do you maintain customer satisfaction for your services?
9. What were the problems you encounter in the implementation process and afterwards?
10. How did you deal with them?
11. What do you think is the most challenging part of 4PL business?
12. How do you deal with that particular challenge?
13. How do you compare your company with other 4PL consultancies?
14. How do you maintain strong relationships with your suppliers?
15. How do you maintain strong relationships with your clients?

Appendix 4: Interview Questions

For the physical service provider- Lightning Source Inc.

1. What is your role in 4PL outsourcing?
2. What do you think is the most challenging part of maintaining 4PL vendor satisfaction?
3. How do you maintain the 4PL vendor satisfaction?
4. How do you meet changing industry trends?
5. What is the most important service that you can provide through 4PL?
6. What are the most important aspects of your relationships with your client?
7. How do you maintain strong relationships with your clients?

Appendix 5: Pattern Matching Table

Elements of Framework	Interview Questions- For the 4PL vendor
Relationship Management and Strategic development	1. Which services do you offer your clients for their overall supply chain management?
	2. What is the most important differentiation (value) that you offer to your clients?
	3. How do you add value to service levels?
	4. What do you think your core competencies are?
	7. How do you meet changing industry trends?
	8. How do you maintain customer satisfaction for your services?
	9. What were the problems you encounter in the implementation process and afterwards?
	10. How did you deal with them?
	11. What do you think is the most challenging part of 4PL business?
	12. How do you deal with that particular challenge?
	13. How do you compare your company with other 4PL consultancies?
	14. How do you maintain strong relationships with your suppliers?
	15. How do you maintain strong relationships with your clients?
4PL Models, Supplier -Client Selection	5. How do you choose your suppliers?
	6. How do you bring relevant parties together to provide the entire service?
Motives for Utilising 4PL	
Drawbacks and Risks of Utilising 4PL	

Appendix 5: Pattern Matching Table

Elements of Framework	Interviewee 1. The 4PL vendor- Director Andrew Latchford
Relationship Management and Strategic development	1. consultancy services.
	2. understanding, integration. The most important point is "detail".
	3. by making it happen and delivering.
	4. EDI integration applicable to situations, an openmind and delivering.
	7. by finding out what is going on in the world, having no preconceptions, reading relevant literature, speaking to people. They think that they drive industry trends by their media coverage.
	8. by talking to the client and the supplier and making them suggestions.
	9. file compatibility issues (file setup).
	10.by following the guidelines in the Lightning Source Inc. website.
	11. marketing and PR.
	12. by being patient and waiting. by trying to deliver what they can, not trying to deliver everything.
	13. others take on every contract even if they cannot deliver solutions, but they only take on contracts that they can deliver solutions for.
	14. with communication.
	15. with communication and giving the best deal available for their clients.
4PL Models, Supplier -Client Selection	5. by understanding what they produce and how they work before they speak to them.
	6. after initial investigation of the potential match between what the client wants and what the supplier can deliver.
Motives for Utilising 4PL	
Drawbacks and Risks of Utilising 4PL	

Appendix 5: Pattern Matching Table

Elements of Framework	Interview Questions- For the client
Relationship Management and Strategic development	11. What are the most important aspects of your relationships with your 4PL suppliers?
	12. How do you maintain strong relationships with your suppliers?
4PL Models, Supplier -Client Selection	8. Why did you choose to utilise 4PL instead of 3PL?
	9. How do you think utilising 4PL adds value to your service?
	10. How did you choose your 4PL supplier?
Motives for Utilising 4PL	1. How has utilising 4PL changed the way you do business?
	2. How has your provision of 4PL changed since you started utilising the service?
	3. How were you encouraged to utilise 4PL services, what were your motives?
Drawbacks and Risks of Utilising 4PL	4. What were the problems you encountered?
	5. Why do you think you encountered those particular problems, and how did you deal with them?
	6. Were there any compatibility issues?
	7. If there were compatibility issues, did you introduce any new applications for your supply chain management?
	13. What are the drawbacks and risks in utilising 4PL services?

Appendix 5: Pattern Matching Table

Elements of Framework	Interviewee 2. The client- CEO Jason Pegler
Relationship Management and Strategic development	11. understanding and communication.
	12. by frequent communication.
4PL Models, Supplier -Client Selection	8. 4PL offered a no risk business with long term exponential growth and global distribution.
	9. with the POD service.
	10. according to what they could deliver, relevant EDI links, price
Motives for Utilising 4PL	1. with less administration duties, better profits and integration of stock.
	2. through 4PL they had product diversity in terms of units and volume and integration.
	3. 4PL provided more time for their core business, less administration duties, better profits, no stock, POD service with global distribution.
	4. learning the ways to setup files.
	5. due to different ways of working.
Drawbacks and Risks of Utilising 4PL	6. Yes, a lot.
	7. They were just careful about file compatibility. They had more than one person to check the final document.
	13. Drawback: slow growth, missing technology links. Risks: There is no risk because they have no excess of stock and the company who owns Lightning Source Inc. is so big.

Appendix 5: Pattern Matching Table

Elements of Framework	Interview Questions- For the physical service provider
Relationship Management and Strategic development	1. What is your role in 4PL outsourcing?
	2. What do you think is the most challenging part of maintaining 4PL vendor satisfaction?
	3. How do you maintain the 4PL vendor satisfaction?
	4. How do you meet changing industry trends?
	5. What is the most important service that you can provide through 4PL?
	6. What are the most important aspects of your relationships with your client?
	7. How do you maintain strong relationships with your clients?
4PL Models, Supplier -Client Selection	
Motives for Utilising 4PL	
Drawbacks and Risks of Utilising 4PL	

Appendix 5: Pattern Matching Table

Elements of Framework	Interviewee 3. The physical service provider- Key account manager Chris Kinsey
	1. POD services, order fulfillment and dispatching for the publishing industry.
	3. by listening to what they are asking for (communication) and POD services.
	5. single copy order fulfillment via multiple channels with global distribution.
Relationship Management and Strategic development	
4PL Models, Supplier -Client Selection	
Motives for Utilising 4PL	
Drawbacks and Risks of Utilising 4PL	

Appendix 5: Pattern Matching Table

Elements of Framework	Interviewee 4. The physical service provider- Client services manager Andrea Mansell
Relationship Management and Strategic development	2. delivering, making sure the deals react with the 4PL vendor, meeting the expectations.
	4. by attending meetings, industry conferences, forums and conducting surveys (questionnaires).
	6. flexibility, client feedback evaluation, customised offers.
	7 with their EDI integration through multiple channels and an openmind.
4PL Models, Supplier –Client Selection	
Motives for Utilising 4PL	
Drawbacks and Risks of Utilising 4PL	

Appendix 5: Pattern Matching Table

Elements of Framework	Summary
	Pattern Matching Summary
Relationship Management and Strategic development	The pattern matching analysis enabled the author to reveal important issues in the theoretical framework, which in this case study were "relationship management and strategic development", "4PL models, supplier- client selection", "motives for utilising 4PL" and "drawbacks and risks of utilising 4PL". Questions about "motives for utilising 4PL" and "drawbacks and risks of utilising 4PL" were only asked to the client because these questions were only relevant for the client. Questions about "4PL models, supplier- client selection" were only asked to the client and the 4PL vendor because these questions were relevant for the client as well as the 4PL vendor. However, questions about "relationship management and strategic development" were asked to all parties in the framework because these were dealing with the issues about relationships, to which all the parties contributed.

Understanding, technology integrated links and delivering were mentioned by all parties about their relationships between each other and about how they maintained strong relationships. The 4PL vendor's most important service was delivering, which was particularly delivered through the physical service provider to the client. It was interesting that Latchford of the VP Group said that delivering was the least challenging part of the business whereas Andrea Mansell of Lightning Source Inc. stated that as the most challenging part. The 4PL vendor brought relevant parties together to provide the entire service by understanding what their suppliers produced and what the clients wanted. Both the physical service provider and the client mentioned POD service with a global distribution |
4PL Models, Supplier -Client Selection	through multiple channels as the most important service they got or provided according to their position. Both the 4PL vendor and the client mentioned file compatibility issues in relation with problems, drawbacks and risks of the 4PL service. A help from both sides along with following the guidelines in the physical service provider's website were mentioned as a solution. Flexibility was important for the 4PL vendor and the physical service provider about
Motives for Utilising 4PL	how they did business. Pegler of Chipmunka mentioned less administration duties, better profits, integration of stock, product diversity in terms of units and volume and a no risk business about the motivation for utilising 4PL services and about how they chose their supplier. He also said that they had a no risk business because the company who owned Lightning Source Inc. was so big. Another important aspect of the relationships mentioned by all parties was communication.
Drawbacks and Risks of Utilising 4PL	